Gallery Books
Editor: Peter Fallon

DOUBLE CROSS

Thomas Kilroy

DOUBLE CROSS

*with a new introduction
by the author*

Gallery Books

This edition of
Double Cross
is first published
simultaneously in paperback
and in a clothbound edition
on 23 September 1994.

The Gallery Press
Loughcrew
Oldcastle
County Meath
Ireland

ISBN 1 85235 147 0 (*paperback*)
    1 85235 148 9 (*clothbound*)

    The Gallery Press receives financial assistance from An Chomhairle Ealaíon / The Arts Council, Ireland.

Characters

WILLIAM JOYCE, known as Lord Haw Haw
BRENDAN BRACKEN, MP, Minister of Information
A FIRE WARDEN
POPSIE, an upper class English lady
LORD CASTLEROSSE, gossip columnist
LORD BEAVERBROOK, proprietor of the *Express* newspapers
MARGARET JOYCE, wife of William Joyce
ERICH, an anglophile German and reader of W. B. Yeats
A LADY JOURNALIST
TWO NARRATORS, one male, one female

The play is written so that it may be played by two actors and an actress. Although time in the play fluctuates, the basic setting is the early 1940s.

Double Cross was first produced by Field Day, in Derry, on 13 February 1986, with the following cast:

WILLIAM JOYCE   Stephen Rea
BRENDAN BRACKEN

NARRATOR   Kate O'Toole
POPSIE
MARGARET JOYCE
A LADY JOURNALIST

NARRATOR   Richard Howard
FIRE WARDEN
LORD CASTLEROSSE
LORD BEAVERBROOK
ERICH

Director: Jim Sheridan
Design: Consolata Boyle
Lighting: Rory Dempster
Film: Thaddeus O'Sullivan

Double Cross opened at the Royal Court Theatre, London, on 10 May 1986.

Introduction

There is no evidence that Brendan Bracken and William Joyce ever met, nor, indeed, that they were ever aware of one another's existence. They are simply part of history's web of ironical possibilities. I've yoked them together in this play so that they might inhabit the one dramatic idea. This is the notion that two men who so spectacularly denied and concealed their native origins might dramatize the deformities of nationalism more effectively than two patriots. I have made them antagonists in the play where they carry out a kind of personal World War II of their own. As in the real World War II, the one on the side of the allies emerges 'victorious' and the one on the side of Nazi Germany comes to a calamitous end. The reason why they end up on either side in the war has nothing to do with where they were born and raised. It has to do, rather, with the driven nature of each man, in each case a personality driven by the compulsion to eliminate, or, if you will, to betray their ancestors. The play tries to undermine the black and white division of all wars, to subvert the righteousness of all political causes and to see the political issues involved through the much more mysterious prism of individual human character. In the play Bracken and Joyce become something like mirror images of one another and they have to be played, of course, by the same actor.

I was also drawn to the stories of these two men for a reason that had nothing to do with politics or ideologies or wars but had to do with the way my own imagination works. This was my interest in doubleness or doubling; that is, the way things repeat themselves endlessly in life or attract their opposites. This is one of the sources of acting or role-playing. It is also behind the universal need to invent stories or alternative realities that may reflect everyday life but that are still distinct from it. This is a play which moves along the line from role-playing at one end to treachery at the other, from fiction-making to political treason. I have always been fascinated by the fact that the act of deception is common to theatricality and criminality.

Bracken in the play is an actor playing out an elaborate part of his own invention on a stage which is at the centre of British power, political and social. Clearly it was a world susceptible to the charm of a master thespian, even if an upstart. Joyce in the play is a creator of dark fictions, driven to this out of a deep, angry impatience with life as it really is. The connection between them is that they are both moved to create alternative lives because the one bequeathed to them at birth was intolerable. This intolerable inheritance, in each case, was Irish.

To surrender to a vision of doubleness is to see much human behaviour (not least, one's own) within a field of irony. There are few images more deflating than the one in the mirror. Nowhere is this irony more powerful than in politics where human behaviour is often at its most crude and simplistic. Take the matter of political oppression. Oppression disables personality. The whole point of oppression is to reduce the person, to remove all potentiality so that control becomes easy. But oppression also profoundly diminishes the oppressor. It may create grotesque distortions in an oppressed culture, inhibiting all kinds of growth, development, change. But it also effects a like rigidity in the invader, the conqueror. There is nothing as calcified as the air of superiority and the ultimate of this is the baleful paralytic stare of the racist.

This play attempts to deal with one kind of mobility, one kind of action across the barriers, the restricting codes that are set up to separate one country from another. Usually such action which cuts across these frontiers is seen as beneficial, contributing to the evolution of the human race, the slow, painful development towards a single human culture. But the action which I've tried to explore here is of another kind and is usually called treason. Treason is one way to reach across a frontier to make contact with the other side. A desperate way, no doubt, and fuelled by the same degree of fervour that keeps the ultra-nationalist going. To base one's identity, exclusively, upon a mystical sense of place, upon the accident of one's birth, seems to me a dangerous absurdity. To dedicate one's life to the systematic betrayal of the same notion seems to me just as absurd.

I wanted to write a play about nationalism and in a real sense *Double Cross* derives from the whole debate about national identity which Field Day did so much to promote in the seventies and eighties. What interested me was not so much nationalism as a source of self-improvement and the advancement of civil rights but nationalism as a dark burden, a source of trauma and debilitation. It was inevitable, then, I suppose, that I sould end up writing about a fascist.

One of the bases of European fascism in this century was a belief in the regenerative powers of the Nation. The Nation in all its purity would restore civilization in a time of crisis. According to fascist thinking in the early decades of the century this was a matter of particular urgency. Everywhere the fascist looked there was evidence of breakdown and sinister threats to what was perceived to be European civilization. Within the culture itself the fascist saw nothing but decay, a massive political and social failure on the part of hedonistic, liberal, middle-class democracy. To the East, waiting to descend upon this ripe prize like a new Gothic invader, were the Marxists. Inside the beleagured gates the fascists saw plenty of fellow-travellers ready to open the gates and let them in.

But the primal force behind fascism was this hatred of the old order with its old world, complacent sophistication, its high culture, its confident sense of its own achievements, its immunity from ordinary concerns. The fascist, the hungry *novus homo*, hated cultivated style and the leisured life, pleasure for the sake of pleasure, artifice for the sake of art. In this, as perhaps in other ways, too, we are reminded that the fascist passion for purification, a burning away of everything but what is seen to be essential, is yet one more bizarre relic of Puritanism in the modern world. There are many sordid roots of anti-semitism but this is one of them, the rage in the ignorant mind against sophisticated style, a style so strongly identified with the Jewish communities of the great European cities between the wars.

The odd thing is that when we now think about fascism the first thing that springs to mind is itself a kind of style. It is as if in destroying everything tainted by high style the fascists were determined to replace it with a declamatory, vulgar style of their own. Hence, the fascist glitz, the couture of uniforms, the literature of propaganda, the choreography of mob and marching automata, the gross monumentalism of the architecture. Real art could only be plundered. As the German armies retreated in defeat from Italy, 22 trucks preceded them, loaded with 532 paintings and 153 sculptures, all loot, a perfect image of the idiocy at the heart of the whole enterprise. Fascist art and not the one it tried to replace can now be seen to be the truly decadent one. As always with attempts to fabricate a populist culture it was deeply offensive towards the people it intended to serve. It denied the capacity of all human kind to appreciate fine things. Fascism represented a triumph of vulgarity based upon rigid control, the same rigidity which informed its politics, its militarism, its theories of race.

I wanted to represent something of this conflict between effete sophistication and fascist brutalism in the conflict between Brendan Bracken and William Joyce, while retaining the threads that I saw binding them together. To this end I even tried to devise two contrasting styles for the two parts of the play. This was particularly so in the scenes between the two men and the two women in their lives because I came to believe that the centre of it all was, finally, psychosexual. It was only at that level that I felt I could humanize the characters below the surface of all that distortion of personality. The style for Bracken is based, parodically, upon the Comedy of Manners while that of Joyce is closer, I hope, to something like Brecht. At any rate, the intention was to formalize the conflict between these two very displaced persons who are, nevertheless, on a like journey. The opposition between England and Germany in the war is but an inscription above their heads, to be grabbed at and held onto, but the fundamental conflicts for both of them are internal.

It is fair to say that *Double Cross* attracted hostility, especially the treatment of sexuality in the lives of the two men. In Ireland I was told by admirers of Lord Haw Haw that the original man would never act in such a fashion towards his wife. In London any depravity on the part of Joyce would have been entirely acceptable. There, however, I was reprimanded for pushing Bracken's dandyism towards kinky sexuality. But, then, after the event, as it were, I received correspondence offering me details of Bracken's sexual tastes that were far more lurid than anything in the play. It's the old problem of trying to fictionalize historical figures. There is always the danger of being unable to compete with the outrageousness of the originals.

All playwrights like to dream of ideal casting, an ideal first production of their work. This is no idle dreaming, however; it is part of the process of playwrighting, of staging the work in one's head. Sometimes you may be fortunate, as I was in this instance, of being able to work from the beginning with a major theatrical artist. *Double Cross* was written for Stephen Rea. It is difficult to convey how much his huge creative energy contributed to the piece.

Thomas Kilroy

Brendan Bracken (1901-58)

1901 **(15 February)** Brendan Bracken born in Templemore, Co. Tipperary. His father, Joseph Bracken, was a prosperous builder, founder member of the Gaelic Athletic Association and a strong supporter of the Republican Movement.

1904 Bracken's father dies.

1908 Family move to Dublin and Brendan sent to school run by Christian Brothers.

1915 A somewhat unruly youth, Bracken sent to a Jesuit boarding school near Limerick. Runs away at the start of the following term. According to a family friend Bracken's mother decides to send him to friends in Australia because he has shown interest in the Irish Republican Youth Movement.

1916 Arrives in the state of Victoria.

1919 Returns to Ireland. His mother, now remarried in Navan, does not welcome him back.

1920 Bracken moves to Lancashire, where he works as a tutor. Combines this with teaching at Collegiate School, where his colleagues believe he is Australian.

(**Autumn**) Enrols as a pupil at Sedbergh, a public school in Cumbria. Gives his date of birth as 14 December 1904, claims to be an orphan. Leaves after a term — but with the 'old school tie'.

1920-21 Movements unclear — held various teaching posts.

1922 Secures a post on the monthly *Empire Review*, an imperialist journal run by a Tory MP.

1923 Bracken meets Winston Churchill, then in his 'wilderness years'. According to Churchill's eldest daughter, Diana, it was presumed Bracken was Churchill's son.

1924 Bracken builds up his business and publishing interests. Appointed to board of publishers Eyre and Spottiswoode.

1928 On behalf of Eyre and Spottiswoode, buys the *Financial News* (later to merge with the *Financial Times*) and *The Economist*).

1929 Adopted as Conservative candidate for North Paddington. Wins by a margin of 528 votes.

1931 Rumoured that Bracken, Churchill, Lloyd George and Sir Oswald Mosley meet to discuss a grand political alliance against the Labour Party. Joyce may also have attended this meeting.

1932 Proposes to Lady Pamela Smith, daughter of the late Earl of Birkenhead, and is turned down. His affections turn to Churchill's god-daughter, Penelope Dudley Ward. Claims he never married because she refused him as well.

1935 A report appears in the *Sunday Express* that Bracken was greatly embarrassed when he had to show his birth certificate. The proprietor, Lord Beaverbrook, sends a reporter to Ireland to investigate Bracken's background.

1939 Becomes Churchill's Parliamentary Private Secretary at the Admiralty.

1940 Churchill appointed Prime Minister of an all-party government. Bracken becomes one of the youngest members of the Privy Council.

1941 Bracken appointed Minister of Information. Defends freedom of the Press and the independent position of the BBC.

1944 *Evening Standard* reproduces a story of 'fifty years ago' from the *Waterford News* that Bracken's father had been refused a gun licence, much to Bracken's fury.

1945 Loses parliamentary seat to Labour.

1947 Bracken stands for the Conservatives in Bournemouth and wins.

1950 Bouts of illness see Bracken cutting down on his business activities. Elected to his 'old school' board of governors at Sedbergh.

1951 Declines post of Colonial Secretary.

1952 Bracken elevated to the peerage as the Viscount Bracken of Christchurch. May have regretted acceptance, and he never took his seat in the Lords.

1958 Bracken diagnosed as having throat cancer, in January. Dies the following August, aged 57 years.

WILLIAM JOYCE (1906-46)

1906 **(24 April)** William Joyce born Brooklyn, New York, of an Irish father and English mother.

1909 Joyce family move to Ireland.

1909-13 Joyce's father becomes a publican in Ballinrobe, Co. Mayo.

1913-21 Joyce family move to Galway, where Michael Joyce becomes a landlord of barracks occupied by the Royal Irish Constabulary.

1918-19 Michael Joyce's property burnt out by Sinn Féin supporters.

1920 William Joyce volunteers as an informer to the RIC.

1921 Joyce arrives in England, ahead of his family. Years later he claims this was due to the fact that his 'intelligence activities' were known to the Irish Republican Army.

1922 Joyce becomes a student at Battersea Polytechnic, studying science.

1923-27 Studies English Language and Literature, and History at Birkbeck College, London University.

1923 Joins British Fascists.

1927 Aged 21, marries Hazel Kathleen Barr, and has two children.

1928 Studies for one year's post-graduate course in Philology.

1928-30 Speaks for and assists Conservative Party.

1933 Applies for British passport.

1933-37 Becomes a member of Sir Oswald Mosley's party, the British Union of Fascists.

1934 Joyce and Mosley acquitted on a charge of riotous assembly.

1936 First marriage dissolved.

1937 Marries Margaret Cairns White, whom he had met at a Fascist meeting. Splits from Mosley and forms the National Socialist League.

1938-39 Charges of assault dismissed in court.

1939 Orders disbandment of National Socialist League. Travels to Germany, with Margaret, one month before war is declared. Joins German Radio. Given the nickname 'Lord Haw Haw' by a *Daily Express* journalist.

1940 Joyce definitely identified by BBC monitors.

1942 Becomes chief commentator on German Radio for English Group. Joyce sues Margaret for divorce, on the grounds of infidelity. She counters with a charge of cruelty. Their divorce is granted. Joyce and Margaret remarry.

1944 Awarded War Service Cross (a civilian award) by Hitler. German passport issued to William Joyce in name of 'Wilhelm Hansen'.

1945 Joyce shot in the leg and arrested by British soldiers on Danish frontier. Flown to London and charged with treason. Claims American citizenship. Convicted and sentenced to death. Appeals to House of Lords. Appeal dismissed.

1946 **(3 January)** William Joyce was hanged at Wandsworth Prison, aged 39.

for Seamus Deane

PART ONE

The Bracken Play: London

Stage left: a living-room dominated by an Adam fireplace with the Romney portait of Edmund Burke above the mantelpiece. A window into the street. A 1940s vintage wireless.

Upstage, flying above the scene, a hanging washing line of larger-than-life figures, cut-out cardboard representations of Churchill, King George V and Sir Oswald Mosley. When these are reversed for Part Two they become: Dr Goebbels, Hitler and Mosley, again.

Downstage, right, a round rostrum which becomes street/roof-top/ broadcasting studio.

Upstage, built into the set, so that it becomes an integral part of the set when it fades, a video/film screen. Before the lights go up there is the sound of an air-raid siren in the distance and then the drone of bombers and distant explosions. The sounds are brought down. Lights up on BRACKEN *in his living-room, twiddling the knobs on the wireless: static, snatches of music, voices, then the clear calling code: 'Germany calling! Germany calling! This is Radio Hamburg and here is William Joyce with a commentary on today's news.'*

JOYCE (*Voice on wireless*) 'Today's report from the German Supreme Command announces the collapse of France. Following the surrender of St Malo and Lorient with over two hundred thousand prisoners, two hundred and sixty aircraft, an armistice has now been signed between Germany and France. My friends, the war in the West is over. After this most mighty victory in German history over the opponents of the greater German Reich, there are no allies left. Only one enemy of Germany remains: England.

BRACKEN *snaps off the wireless and walks about.*

BRACKEN That's William Joyce, you know. Known as Lord Haw Haw. Could never understand why they call him that. A jumped-up little fascist from the Irish Free State. Sounds more like backstreet Brixton or Kilburn on a Saturday night, wouldn't you say? Actually, I only listen to the filthy little traitor as part of my job. As Minister of Information in His Majesty's Government I do have to listen to a lot of tommyrot, I'm afraid.

He turns on the wireless again.

JOYCE Now is the time for all loyal Britons to call upon the government to resign, at once, to prevent further, useless slaughter. To rid ourselves of the warmonger Churchill and his craven supporters, the gangster Beaverbrook and that well known poseur and parasite, Mr Brendan Bracken —

He turns off wireless again.

BRACKEN Did you ever? Did you hear that? The nerve! Not going to listen to another word. Bloody twit. Knew the fellow well, you know, before he turned traitor with the Nazis. Vulgar little shit from Connemara, full of fight, ready to take on anyone. You know the kind of Paddy. Joined Tom Mosley's blackshirts. British Union of Fascists, that is. Tom eventually had to throw him out. Constantly beating up yids in the East End. The Irish are always being thrown out of something or other, aren't they? I'm absolutely convinced he's over there in Berlin, now, simply to be in the middle of the row. Coat off, sleeves up and bejasus we're off. Dreadful chap, actually.

JOYCE *appears on the video/film screen: black shirt, tie.* BRACKEN *affects a studied indifference.*

JOYCE My friends, let me introduce the kind of crony who hangs around Churchill. Take this specimen of outrageous masquerade, Mr Brendan Bracken, MP, Minister of Information, would you believe!

BRACKEN I'm not listening. I'm not paying the slightest attention to any of this —

JOYCE Who is this Brendan Bracken? Who is this creature who pretends to be a member of the English establishment? I can tell you, my friends. He's the son of a Tipperary stonemason who was also a dynamite terrorist. He arrived in England with a cheque book, wangled his way into a minor public school for one year, memorized Burke's peerage and back issues of the *Empire News* so that he knew the genealogy of every decent home in the country and the name of every significant clergyman in the Church of England. In this way he name-dropped his way to the top of the heap —

BRACKEN Of course, Mosley did attract all the oddballs.

JOYCE And this is the kind of man who now stands beside Churchill! Is it any wonder that England is in the most troubled phase of her history?

BRACKEN All marching about with stiff elbows and that constipated swagger of the Hun. Disgruntled grocers from Battersea, proponents of cock-fighting in Norfolk —

JOYCE Don't be misled, my friends, by the clownish demeanour of this man!

BRACKEN Vegetarian old lady fascists from Sussex who would skewer a comma with one of their knitting needles —

JOYCE Remember this is the man who is the confidant of Churchill. This is the man who controls Fleet Street. This is the man who censors and determines the flow of information to the British people during this quite unnecessary war.

BRACKEN The question is, though: how did this chappie Joyce end up as Dr Goebbels' right-hand man on the wireless?

JOYCE The question is, what does it say about democracy if such a trickster can rise to the top?

BRACKEN Lord Haw Haw, I ask you!

JOYCE Mr Brendan Bracken, Tory MP for North Paddington, of all places!

BRACKEN The traitor!

JOYCE The trickster!

> ACTOR *and* ACTRESS *forward in anonymous coats, to either side of the stage.*

ACTOR (*Narrator*) Ladies and gentlemen, this is the story of two men who invented themselves.

ACTRESS (*Narrator*) When a man wipes out his past and invents his own future he may have criminal or artistic tendencies.

ACTOR On the other hand he may be simply acting out a condition of the culture from which he is trying so desperately to escape.

ACTRESS Both men left Ireland in the twenties.

ACTOR At the precise time when Ireland declared its independence of England.

ACTRESS In England they both obliterated all evidence of their Irishness. Fabricating, instead, ultra-English identities for themselves.

ACTOR When the bombs began to fall over Western Europe after 1939 Bracken was in London, by Churchill's side, Joyce was in Berlin, on the other side of the fence.

ACTRESS Before he died, Bracken had created modern British financial journalism —

ACTOR Chairman of the *Financial Times* Group —

ACTRESS Elevated to the peerage —

ACTOR Although he never entered the House of Lords which he insisted upon calling the geriatric clinic —

BRACKEN (*Suddenly taking over*) Actually, I died of cancer. (*Indicating throat*) Somewhere about here. If you were to put your hand there, you would feel — Now, look here. Before there's any more nonsense

I simply wanted to say that I suffered one particular libel all my life. That I was the illegitimate son of Sir Winston. By the by, have you noticed how people quicken at the prospect of unexpected cash or alternatively scandal among the notabilities? The whole British newspaper industry is based upon the satisfaction of those twin appetites. As for the Churchill bastardy, why should I deny it if people were prepared to indulge such a biological-historical impossibility? Randolph the cad was responsible for the innuendo. Trotting around the Savoy referring loudly to me as 'my bastard brother Brendan'. Do you think it might be merely the appeal of the alliteration? I replaced him, you see. Winston was, always will be, a father to me. (*Bright change*) Actually, my father was a bishop, don't you know, on the Cape —

ACTRESS Correction!

BRACKEN And that's another thing. (*Indicating the figure*) This fellow Joyce. Never met the chap. I want to make that perfectly clear, because you will hear otherwise later on.

JOYCE (*Eruption*) *Wir habt doch gesiegt!**

BRACKEN He'll go on like that for hours if he's allowed —

JOYCE This is not defeat.

BRACKEN He's referring to the Hitler War, you know.

JOYCE (*Rush-power*) As I face my Lord Jesus, I am purged of all impurity. The clean eye sees beyond this imperfection of limbs, this vale of tears, this habitat of the Jew plutocrat and his lickspittle protectors in high places. My friends, keep worthy company. Leave the shallow to the shallow and the nidering to the nidering. Keep thine eye on the sword in the rooftree. In death as in life I defy the Jew-boy who is responsible for this late war. I defy the Power of Darkness in the Jew-pig. I pray to Almighty God that England will be great again. May the standard of the Hakenkreutz be raised from the dust! I call on the dead sons of England who have died without knowing

*Colloquial, We have won!

25

why. I call on their seed that the future generations of England may ensure the nobility of the
race! *Sieg Heil! Sieg Heil! Sieg Heil!* (*Bows head*)

ACTRESS William Joyce was hanged for high treason,
January 3rd 1946, at Wandsworth Prison, and his
body was buried in quicklime.

ACTOR Thirty years later still, the Joyce family brought
the remains back, for interment, to Galway from
where young William had fled in 1922 in the wake
of the retreating British Army and the Black and
Tans. You might say he was always a few strides
behind marching feet.

Lights out on JOYCE.

BRACKEN Actually, he was American this chap, Joyce. That's
why we had such trouble hanging him. Mustn't
hang a Yank. Not in 1946, at any rate. Actually, the
future is with the Englishness, not England, I'm
afraid. The whole world will be divided between
those who speak the language and those who
don't. Can't imagine what the other lot will
look like. Probably slanted eyes and indifferent
pigmentation, wouldn't you say. It's obscene,
that's what I said to Winston, it's obscene that this
creature Joyce should claim to speak for England
from the scaffold. Then Winston said rather a
curious thing. My dear, he said, we have always
taken more captives with our dictionaries than
with our regiments.

ACTRESS When *he* died in 1958, Bracken's throat had closed
over the tubes through which they had tried to
feed him. At the express wish of the deceased
there was no funeral, no memorial service.

ACTOR You could say that he had died of the one thing
calculated to kill him. Speechlessness.

Lights out on BRACKEN.

ACTRESS Ladies and gentlemen! We cannot vouch for the

accuracy of anything that is going to follow —

ACTOR Even of what is verifiable in the history books —

ACTRESS It has been put together to make a point.

ACTOR Question: What is the difference between an Irishman's need to conceal his Irishness and an Englishman's need to believe in the concealment?

ACTRESS Question: What is the connection between the Germanic love of English literature and the success of Dr Goebbels' radio propaganda?

ACTOR Put another way: Why does the victim always try to imitate the oppressor?

ACTRESS Women are well aware of this condition.

ACTOR Men only discover it when they are political underdogs.

ACTRESS Imitate that you may be free.

ACTOR There is also the momentum of colonialism which operates like an inverted physics.

ACTRESS The further out on the periphery, the stronger the pull to the centre.

ACTOR Every metropolis is thronged with provincials.

ACTRESS Each trying to be more metropolitan than the other. And so, to play!

She bows and exits.

ACTOR Let us begin then with Mr Bracken in full flight upon his favourite instrument of communication, the telephone.

He exits. Sounds of frantic telephone ringing. Down to: BRACKEN, *standing, holding, in turn, a variety of telephone receivers.*

BRACKEN (*Phone*) Hello? Hello! I wish to speak with Lady Colefax, if you please. (*Short pause*) Certainly not. I haven't the slightest interest in addressing her appointments' secretary. (*Pause*) And do be quick about it, there's a dear. (*Off phone*) Bloody cow! (*Phone*) Sybil! Darling! That was a delightful Thursday. (*Pause*) Yes, well, that woman *is* a gorgon. If I may say so, you displayed the patience of Job before her antics. (*Pause*) Absolutely. (*Pause*) Absolutely. (*Impatient pause*) Absolutely. Nothing could improve her short of major surgery. Now, *The Economist*, Sybil darling. (*Pause*) Don't you remember? *The Economist.* You did promise — I simply want to be able to tell the banker chappies that you are willing to sell your holding to me. (*Pause*) Yes, I know it's all such a perfect bore but you know how I have dedicated my life to the elimination of boredom. (*Ho-ho*) (*New phone*) Charles? That you? The old sweetheart is prepared to sell. (*Pause*) Never mind how. Make it fifty thousand, would you. (*Pause*) What? How much? (*Pause*) Seventy thousand? Who is behind this bid? (*Pause*) Oh, he is, is he? Not to worry. I'll deal with him. (*Pause*) Well, I happen to know that he happens to think that I may be advising on the Civil List. Mum's the word! (*New phone*) Reggie? You can get your knickers out of a twist, dear. We're there. We now control the *Banker*, the *Financial News* and the *Investors Chronicle. The Economist* will be the stone at the centre of the pendant, as it were. (*Pause*) Of course it's my own phrase, you idiot. By the by, who were those gorgeous people with the Duff Coopers last night? (*Pause*) Really? I'd adore meeting them anon if you can arrange it. Knew their son well at Oxford, as a matter of fact. Splendid fellow. (*Pause*) Well, Balliol, as a matter of fact. (*Pause*) Well, you bloody well know now, don't you! (*Off phone*) That superannuated shit! (*New phone*) Eddie? Couldn't get back before this. Got your message at White's. Glad to be of help. (*Pause*) Where exactly is your boy in the clink? (*Pause*) Ah, Marseilles! Know it well. Not to worry. No one worries about such peccadillos nowadays. I'll get the FO on to it first thing in the morning. Better still, let me get the brother on to it. Terribly well connected with the Frogs, the brother. Import-export, that sort of thing. He'll know exactly what to do about a prison. By the by, you do know the Bishop of Durham, don't you? Want to have a word with him, if you can set it up. (*Pause*) Well, actually, it's about the Canterbury Succession. (*Pause*) My dear man, the future of the Church is as dear to me as is the Empire. Anyway, old Cosmo Lang Swine hasn't much longer to go. Terribly important to have the right man in that particular post in these troubled times. I am, after all, the publisher of the *Book of Common Prayer*, you know. Besides, my father was a — a distinguished clergyman. Didn't know that, did you, now? (*New phone; entirely different tone: hurt, vulnerable*) You didn't call. I sat by the phone. (*Pause*) All night. (*Outburst*) It is not casual to me. (*Pause*) Sorry. I do not mean it as an obligation, either. (*Pause*) Well, we do not have to call it love, do we. Yes. Very well. Good night, Popsie. (*New phone; again an entirely different tone: cold anger*) It's you, is it? You must never, never, never telephone me again, do you hear! I will pay your demands. I will continue to pay your lousy demands. I will do this not because of your threats and bullying, no, because I despise such threats, but I will pay you because of our mother, because you are my brother but never again, here or anywhere else, are you to dare to telephone me.

Long pause. Shaken. Conscious effort at recovery.
Last phone call, a call to arms.

Winston! (*Pause*) Yes, well, I did hear rumours, actually. Yes. Yes. Yes. Minister of Information. Yes. Absolutely wonderful, great honour, of course. (*Pause*) You know my feelings, Winston, from the House. This war must be conducted in public. The press is one of our strongest weapons. Especially since the Hun is incapable of calling upon the same ally. (*Pause*) Yes, well I've talked to

Max. And the Berrys. And Esmond Harmsworth. (*Pause*) Well, you know, if you wish to control the press you talk to owners, not editors, my dear. Yes —

End of phones. BRACKEN *stands to attention before a hidden authority.*

The Right Honourable Minister of Information (*Testing the words*) Brendan Bracken, MP, Member for North Paddington. (*Pause: fresh start*) Viscount Bracken of . . . Pretoria? No. Hobart? Viscount Bracken of Hobart? No. Christchurch. Ah! Viscount Bracken of Christchurch. (*Stiffening*) In this terrible war, I will serve my country and my king against the forces of darkness which threaten our very civilization —

To POPSIE *in a peignoir at the edge of* BRACKEN's *room.* BRACKEN *is within, fiddling with the wireless so that she is able to look in at him from without.*

POPSIE (*To audience*) I loved being with him at times like that. He gave the impression of having composed the whole thing in his head, as if he had written the book in which all the important people were characters of his imagination. But how could one possibly give oneself wholly to someone who was never there, if you see what I mean?

She disrobes to a Boy Scout uniform beneath the peignoir.

He needed costuming to become sexually — you know. Hence my Baden-Powell outfit. Windswept hair on the uplands, jolly boys in tents. That kind of thing, I suppose.

BRACKEN Popsie! Popsie! Come here! I've got the little bugger.

POPSIE *steps into the room. Stops, hands on hips.*

POPSIE Oh, God, Brendan, not more of that boring shit.
Please.

BRACKEN Listen!

JOYCE (*On wireless, up*) Germany calling! Germany
calling! Here are the stations: Calais One, 514
metres, Calais Two, 301.6 metres, Köln, 456
metres, Breslau, 316 metres and the short-wave
transmitter DXX, 48.86 metres. And now, with a
commentary on the news, William Joyce —

BRACKEN The filthy little traitor with the vulgar voice —

POPSIE (*Caught*) Shh!

JOYCE (*On wireless*) Tonight, the Luftwaffe will give
London a taste of what is to come if this war is
not brought to a swift conclusion. One hundred
and forty bombers will devastate the City of
London —

BRACKEN Liar!

JOYCE (*On wireless*) Direct reprisal for the indiscriminate
bombing of German citizens by the RAF, old men,
women and children under the orders of the arch-
murderer, Churchill. But Mr Churchill can no
longer hide behind his cigar —

BRACKEN *snaps off the wireless and stands, shaking.*

POPSIE If you find him so utterly repulsive, why do you
insist upon listening to him, night after night?
Really, Brendan!

She lies on the sofa and puts her legs up. BRACKEN,
in tension, turns on the wireless again.

JOYCE (*On wireless*) — our fleet in the North Sea.
Meanwhile, Churchill's minion, Churchill's choir-
boy, Churchill's ingle, one Mr Brendan Bracken,
fumes in Whitehall. According to the High
Command, over one hundred thousand gross
tonnage of shipping has been sunk in the North

Atlantic by —

> BRACKEN, *in a fury, switches off the wireless again.*

BRACKEN Did you hear that?
POPSIE How can I hear if you insist on turning it off?
BRACKEN He referred to me!
POPSIE Rubbish.

> BRACKEN *is now back at the wireless but all that comes out is a Victor Sylvester-style waltz and, then, a whole variety of stations.*

Brendan! Turn that bloody thing off! At once! Brendan!

> BRACKEN *obeys, switches off the wireless, buries his head in his hands.*

Brendan. Are you all right?
BRACKEN (*Sudden alertness, sudden control*) Of course. I'm perfectly fine, thank you. I refuse to think about him anymore. Here. Come sit on my knee, Popsie.
POPSIE Like this?
BRACKEN Forward a little. Hold it. Ah!
POPSIE Do you think you're making love to a boy?
BRACKEN Certainly not. How could I? What a question.
POPSIE It's simply one of the things which might occur to a casual observer of this delicate scene.
BRACKEN How boringly literal of you, my dear.
POPSIE The question is: are we proceeding to the inner sanctum or is this to be prolonged dalliance in the outer chambers?
BRACKEN Who would want anything else with the pleasure of such a — such a — composition?
POPSIE Speak for yourself.
BRACKEN It's the image, my dear. What might otherwise be beyond our reach. I wonder if that's what it's all about? The contrivance of what is really

inaccessible?

POPSIE What? Sex?

BRACKEN No. Art. Well, both as a matter of fact.

POPSIE Do you not feel anything? There?

BRACKEN Not a thing, I'm afraid.

POPSIE Perhaps I should change into my Highland tartan? Or my gymslip? Or my Florence Nightingale? I shouldn't object in the least if you had a boy. I'd find it jolly exciting, as a matter of fact. I mean there is always a certain rub-off, isn't there, between lovers?

> BRACKEN *extricates himself, firmly, and leaves her sitting on the sofa.*

What on earth are you doing?

BRACKEN I'm re-arranging myself.

POPSIE So I see.

BRACKEN You always do it, Popsie. Ruining everything with your pedestrian specifics —

POPSIE I have to say what is what. I can't abide unreality. It's downright immoral. I was brought up to believe what is is and what is not is not.

BRACKEN How can one give oneself to a dream, an image —

POPSIE Besides, what is really bothering you is sexual truth — you spend your life constantly evading, constantly avoiding, constantly inventing — How can one possibly live like that?

BRACKEN You're just a common little tart!

POPSIE And you're just a twisted little Irish puritan!

BRACKEN Whore!

POPSIE Oh, dear, we're beginning to sound like South Americans.

BRACKEN I can't abide lewd talk! You know that.

POPSIE For Heaven's sake, can you not be yourself for once! You conceal nothing from me, Brendan, nothing, and it doesn't make the slightest difference to my feeling for you, whatever you are. Don't you see that? (*Cry*) Well, why can't you trust me, then?

BRACKEN   Tell you what, Popsie! Let's dash off to the country for the weekend!

POPSIE   (*To the world*) I give up. Truly. I give up.

BRACKEN   Give some of our friends a tinkle —

POPSIE   A: There's a war on. B: There's no petrol. C: I never wish to see that appalling car of yours, that Hispano Suiza with its garish blue carriage lamps, ever again, in this lifetime.

BRACKEN   We had jolly times, didn't we?

POPSIE   No. Yes, it was fun. The problem is I no longer see myself in the situation. Perhaps one needs to distance oneself from roguery in order to enjoy it.

BRACKEN   Freedom is distance, actually. Beaverbrook once said that to me. Freedom is distance, is space, Bracken. Never forget that, Bracken. We live in the one country in the world which respects that space as a matter of its very definition as a nation, as a civilized culture. That every man should have space between him and another. That every State should have space between it and its neighbour. That's what old Max said. (*Reflectively*) Every tinpot revolutionary from the year dot has dreamed of that space, that hiving-off of another, the Other, some tyrannical shadow, some dark father, and for what? For the brief space before the space is filled again and one begins again, again and again, for freedom, over and over again before one's morning shaving-mirror.

POPSIE   I would never have thought Max Aitken capable of the perception.

BRACKEN   Oh, I have embroidered upon the relatively simple-minded headline of dear Max. *Daily Express*, y'know.

POPSIE   I am sure you have.

BRACKEN   It's odd, isn't it, that patriotism and treason may be fuelled by the same hunger for space —

POPSIE   You are quite incorrigible, Brendan.

BRACKEN   But then all things are opposites of other things as my old chum Willy Yeats would say.

POPSIE   Brendan — have you listened to even one word of

what I've said?

BRACKEN What? What do you mean?

POPSIE Every time I try to reach you, yet another Brendan Bracken is talked into existence. Like a distracting mushroom. Very disconcerting.

BRACKEN I happen to subscribe to the Wildean notion that one must make of one's life a work of art. We're given pretty dismal material to start with. One must shape it into significance. I believe that that's what's meant by salvation.

POPSIE For God's sake, I'm talking about ordinary, basic, human feeling! I love you, Brendan.

BRACKEN And I love you, too.

POPSIE I know that that is the signal for us not to see one another for a while.

BRACKEN Yes.

POPSIE (*Hope*) Perhaps, if you could just put that past behind you —

BRACKEN I am an orphan!

POPSIE Balderdash!

BRACKEN Like every other orphan I've been travelling all my life towards some closed door. When it opens I expect someone to walk through. Someone whom I shall instantly recognise.

POPSIE For Heaven's sake, Brendan, we all know perfectly well that you're not an orphan.

BRACKEN I am an orphan!

POPSIE You've had those perfectly normal, nice Irish parents of yours back in the land of the shamrock. I mean, what more does one need?

BRACKEN Orphanhood, my dear, may be as much a condition of choice as an unhappy product of the Great Reaper.

POPSIE Sometimes, I truly believe that you contrive subjects for conversation simply in order to match phrases which you have already formed in your head.

BRACKEN I never leave anything to chance.

POPSIE Obviously not.

BRACKEN Especially not the language.

POPSIE Well, I must say I have never known anyone to use the English language quite in the way that you do, Brendan.

BRACKEN Why not?

POPSIE Well, it's rather as if one were speaking to someone who was discovering the words as he went along. It's aboriginal, extremely refreshing, of course —

BRACKEN (*He means it*) That is the most appalling thing anyone has ever said to me.

POPSIE What's the matter?

BRACKEN Insulting! Denigrating!

POPSIE What is?

BRACKEN Forget it. That's enough.

POPSIE What is the matter with you? You become upset at the most trivial things.

BRACKEN Trivial!

POPSIE I haven't an earthly idea of what all the fuss is about.

BRACKEN You call my use of the language trivial!

POPSIE Of course. One opens one's mouth and words come out. Perfectly straightforward I should say.

BRACKEN It is what makes me what I am! Without it, I am nothing!

She has considerable difficulty with this.

POPSIE Are you in pain again with that throat of yours?

BRACKEN Of course I'm in pain. I'm in pain every time my sensibility is outraged by a gross version of reality.

POPSIE I didn't quite mean that, Brendan. How is your throat?

BRACKEN Most days I am reduced to semolina and porridge. Not at the same time, of course. Every human person has his flowering blight. Mine just happens to be here. That is all.

POPSIE You shouldn't be alone.

BRACKEN You have an extraordinary aptitude, my dear, for the essential statement.

POPSIE Very well. If you must be swinish about it I'm going to trot along. (*No response*) I expect I had better get this ridiculous uniform off, hadn't I? Can't go out dressed like this.

BRACKEN No. One should always be appropriately dressed for the outdoors.

> BRACKEN *goes, peers through the curtains into the street. She gives up on him and turns to go.*

POPSIE Oh, blast! I've gone and ripped these bloody shorts again! Heavens! How I've put on weight!

> *She goes out leaving* BRACKEN *by the window. Light held on* BRACKEN *a moment and then down. Meanwhile, light on the actor as* LORD CASTLEROSSE, *in an armchair, downstage right. He is dressed in a grossly padded kaftan and a floppy tasselled Turkish fez, a heavy fat man who can scarcely breathe under his own weight.*

CASTLEROSSE (*To audience*) To understand Bracken, you see, you must go back to before the war. Actually Bracken's Irish past was never much of a mystery to the rest of us. Mentioned it meself, oodles of times, in me gossip column in *The Sunday Express*.

Mr Brendan Bracken, the flamboyant Celt, was at Sybil Colefax's last Thursday. You couldn't go to a party without bumping into him, a red-haired golliwog wearing indifferent suits. Bloody marvellous company, though. The thing about the English is that they're too damned polite to ask who you are or where you're from. So what, anyway, I say, if the feller is getting on with it. He was running five newspapers by the time he was thirty. Including the *Financial News* and *The Economist*. Don't think he knew a damned thing about business, any more than the rest of us. I once asked him what was the secret of international banking. He said: a mastery of Slavic monosyllables, m'dear. What a glorious scoundrel he was, dear Brendan.

I'm supposed to tell you about Beaverbrook though. Beaverbrook wanted to know about Bracken. Beaverbrook wanted to know about everyone. Kept secret files on people. In a bloody big box. Called it his Deadman's Chest.

Any rate. There was Max on the phone. Sometime in the early thirties. I say, Castlerosse, you're Irish, you'll enjoy this. I *am* Irish, actually, meself. Earl of Kenmare, 's matter of fact. Last of the line. There you are. Got a bit of a family seat over in County Kerry. Trying to turn the bloody place into a golf course at present. Bloody marvellous country for golf courses, Ireland.

Any rate. There was Max, bubbling with gossip as usual. You'll get a charge out of this, old Max said. What's that, Max, I said. Bracken's father, he said. Bracken's father was a damned Fenian, he said. The police in Dublin Castle had a mug-shot of the old geezer on display. Notorious felon. Blowing up places. That kind of thing. What Max had done, you see, was sent over one of his investigator fellers from the *Daily Express* to Ireland where the whole sorry tale was laid bare by the vindictive natives.

You're Irish, Valentine, Max said, what d'you think of that? Well, Max, I said, there are Irish and there are Irish and then there are other Irish. Max didn't quite get the point. Canadian, y'see. Actually, I adored Brendan. He had that splendid Irish neck, if you see what I mean. Bit nouveau, perhaps. I mean to say there was that ludicrous business of his buying that four-poster bed. Couldn't get the thing into that bloody house in North Street. Bed abandoned, apparently.

He invited Willy Yeats, once, down for the weekend to Freddy Britton-Austin's house. Pretending the house was his own. The Britton-Austins were abroad, d'you see. He even gave Yeats a book out of the library as a memento of the visit. Yeats went off, muttering and mumbling, thrilled with the hospitality. An absolute scoundrel, Brendan, but glorious fun.

What Beaverbrook wanted to find out, you see, was where did Bracken stand in the general huffle. A bloody awful time, the thirties. The cat could have jumped either way. Everyone was having secret meetings. Winston and his lot, Beaverbrook and his Imperialists, Bracken bobbing up and down between them, Mosley and his gang of unemployed clerks and county types. All yelling and shouting about the fate of England. Everyone thought at the time that the only problem with Hitler was that he was frightfully common. It was only later realized, as they say in the movies, that it was him or us. Brendan had had himself elected as a Tory MP for North Paddington, of all places. What Max wanted to know, y'see, was which kind of Irishman was he, the kind who went high on the swing-boats or the kind who took potshots in the shooting gallery.

(*Shift in tone*) Of course the Irish are always trying to be something other than Irish or else they're being more Irish than you could possibly believe. Dreadful people, really. Glad to be out of the place. So was Bracken. He never talked about it, though. The only thing I ever remember him saying about Ireland was that his mother had suffered there. But I never got that particular story —

He meditates upon this as the lights come down on him. A few brass pieces play 'Hearts of Oak' and 'Rule Britannia'. A Union Jack and Tory streamers float down before the cardboard cut-out figures of Churchill, the King and Mosley. BRACKEN *is on a high platform waving to the crowds who shout and heckle. A rehearsed chorus from somewhere:* 'Bracken for Britain', 'Bracken for Britain'.

Hecklers: 'What about the millions on the dole, then?' Chorus of 'Rule Britannia'.

CHAIRMAN (*Voiceover on loudspeaker*) Ladies and gentlemen of the great Borough of Paddington, may I introduce the Conservative candidate for the constituency. He comes from British-Irish stock and was born in Bedfordshire, the son of a distinguished officer in the Indian Army. He has one residence in London, one in Bedfordshire, with estates in Scotland and Northern Ireland. An old Sedbergh boy and a distinguished graduate in History from Oxford University — Mr Brendan Bracken!

Cheers, cat-calls and wild trumpet playing.

BRACKEN (*Stilling the crowd*) May I say, that there can be little wrong with England when her sons and daughters can raise their voices in joyful unison in such good old English songs. (*Jeers*) Fellow Britons! We are here today, under the Crown and flag, to rid this city, this nation, once and for all, of the socialist menace, to expose the slobbery promises of MacDonald and Henderson and all their Bolshevik tribe! (*Uproar*) Let me make one thing perfectly clear. No man has a greater respect for the English working man than I. No one knows better than I, how our great Empire is founded upon the decent English labouring classes. But we are not talking about native sons of England, my friends. We are talking about foreign poison which is seeping into our system. Do we want to be controlled by the Moscow Comintern? Are we to be ruled by a gang of Russian malcontents and perverts? Do we want our government clumping around the Palace in suits rented from Moss Brothers? (*Laughter. Yell: 'Why not, ya bleedin' twit?'*) If there is one thing that has always been true in this great land of ours, it is respect for our leaders. (*Yell: 'Go and march with Mosley's blackshirts, then!'*) My friend, I'm glad you said that. Thank you, my friend. Thank you for allowing me to say that I respect the rights of Englishmen to walk the streets of England behind the Union Jack. I do not hold with anti-Semitism. No. But neither do I think, my friends, that our country should be over-run by alien races, the riff-raff of Russia, the refuse of the dens of the East — (*Hands aloft to uproar of cheers and boos*)

> *The lights fade. A voice singing in darkness:*
> *'I fear no foe with Thee at hand to bless.*
> *Ills have no weight, and tears no bitterness.'*
> *Light-up on* BEAVERBROOK *behind a small desk on the rostrum. Tight, small body in a black suit, white shirt, black tie. Great, balding head, tufted eyebrows, glasses on nose.*

BEAVERBROOK (*With papers*) 'Where is death's sting, where grave thy victory? I triumph still if thou abide with me.'

SERVANT (*Voice off*) Lord Beaverbrook! Lord Beaverbrook! Sorry to bother you, lord!

BEAVERBROOK What is it, Arthur?

SERVANT (*Off*) Mr Bracken, lord. He wants a word with you. Says it's urgent.

BEAVERBROOK Always is, with Brendan. Show him up, Arthur. (*Undertone*) Better get this damn well right first go.

> *Sounds off: Door opening; door closed.* BRACKEN *steps up before* BEAVERBROOK.

BRACKEN That it should come to this, Max.

BEAVERBROOK Use the vernacular, Brendan.

BRACKEN You're a shit, Max.

BEAVERBROOK Hope that makes you feel better, Brendan.

BRACKEN I would never dream of doing such a thing to a friend.

BEAVERBROOK Baloney!

BRACKEN Utterly without scruple —

BEAVERBROOK Don't give me that Holy Joe act, Brendan. It won't wash.

BRACKEN Violating my privacy.

BEAVERBROOK Look! It's simple. I sent a man over to Ireland. I said to him: Check out Bracken. I want to know everything possible about his background. Off he went. Nearly got bogged down in Dublin *en route*. But eventually he got as far as Templemore, Co. Tipperary. And was told the full story of Brendan Bracken. It's here. Over there. In an evelope. In a drawer.

BRACKEN I see. And what do you propose to do? With this envelope?

BEAVERBROOK Nothing. *Rien*. Forget about it.

BRACKEN And you ask me to believe that you —

BEAVERBROOK I'm a journalist, Brendan. I chase stories.

BRACKEN I would never do such a thing to you —

BEAVERBROOK Well, it's about bloody time you did. Go on. Go get a file on me. Then we'll be quits. The basis of a perfect relationship.

BRACKEN Relationship!

BEAVERBROOK Certainly. Based upon reality. Based upon facts and figures and not some sentimental tosh. My dear Brendan, I dislike your nanny sensitivity. It is the least agreeable side of your make-up. Besides, it's phoney. You only pull that act when you're caught on the hop. You see, what you're ignoring in all this, what you're forgetting, my friend, is that I admire you immensely. All the more because of the contents of that envelope, I might add. We're both questors, Brendan. We've both come in from the frontier. We know what the fight is all about because we've looked into the wilderness. The jungle out there —

BRACKEN I had nothing — absolutely nothing —

BEAVERBROOK They don't know about such things here on the mainland, Brendan. Especially not those titled asses in the Lords.

BRACKEN I had to begin. From the very beginning.

BEAVERBROOK When I arrived here from Montreal thirty years ago, the first thing I did was buy a Rolls-Royce. The second thing I did was decide to buy the Rolls-Royce company. Which I did.

BRACKEN I was unfree. Every day of my childhood I would say: Tomorrow, tomorrow I'm going to be free.

BEAVERBROOK You know why I could do all this? Sure we have a free marketplace back home. But this was different. This was free entry into the most complex civilization since the Romans. This was the sign of belonging. You talk about freedom? Think of the freedom of that. And why? Why because I am British. You're British. We believe in the Empire. We believe in the greatest compromise between democracy and élitism ever devised by human political ingenuity.

BRACKEN You know, I used to imagine, as a little boy, that people didn't recognise me, that I appeared to everyone as a stranger. I used to pretend not to recognise my name when it was called.

BEAVERBROOK The problem with you, Brendan, is that you think you can invent the future. You can't. You can only master it when it does happen.

BRACKEN I want no one to see these papers, Max.

BEAVERBROOK That's the difference between you and me, Brendan. That's the reason why you'll never make money.

BRACKEN You've heard me, Max. I don't want anyone to read that file.

BEAVERBROOK My dear Brendan, you're missing the whole point. People would respect you for what you've done. The Englishman always respects the man who comes in from the colonies. Always has. Always found a place for him. New blood. New energy. Men tempered by the fire at the front. Men who make the choice.

BRACKEN I want no one else to see these papers, Max.

BEAVERBROOK What the hell's the matter with you, man?

BRACKEN (*Outburst*) All that is dead! I want nothing to do with what was! I cannot be what I am if I'm saddled with that!

BEAVERBROOK You can forget it. It's past.

BRACKEN For God's sake, that isn't enough! It must be totally suppressed.

BEAVERBROOK *slowly opens a drawer in the desk. Removes an envelope. Removes papers from the envelope. Reads.*

BEAVERBROOK 'Date of birth: February 15th, 1901.'

BRACKEN I was born in the British Empire.

BEAVERBROOK Yeah. Sure. Irish Free State didn't exist then.

BRACKEN And since the place in which I was born chose to break its connection with the Crown by force, I never wish to be associated with it, ever again.

BEAVERBROOK So? What's the problem? There is no problem. My dear boy, history has been uncommonly generous to you. You should seize upon it as a sign, a charm that few are blessed with. History allowed you to choose. How many more can you say the same of down the centuries?

BRACKEN 'To be bred in a place of estimation, to see nothing low or sordid from one's infancy — to be habituated in the pursuit of honour and duty — '

BEAVERBROOK Eh? What's that?

BRACKEN Edmund Burke on the British inheritance.

BEAVERBROOK Ah. You know Gandhi once quoted Edmund Burke at me. You know — the Indian. The one who wants to dismantle the Empire. Do you know Gandhi, Brendan?

BRACKEN (*Sudden turn so that it shocks* BEAVERBROOK *and drains* BRACKEN) I don't need to know him. I know his type. That sanctimonious, ascetic face with its watery eyes, running with pious self-denial. Peasants in the fields. What an image for the world to imitate! I despise him, begging bowl in one hand, dagger concealed in the other. Determined to prove the superiority of the primitive. I would happily trample him into the ground. What do these people know of law? Of grace?

Cultivated living? They would overrun us, mark you. With their foul smells. Their obscene rituals. Animalism.

BEAVERBROOK OK, OK, OK. Calm down. Here, sit. It's OK.

BRACKEN I'm sorry.

BEAVERBROOK You want a brandy?

BRACKEN No. No.

BEAVERBROOK We have to soldier together, Brendan, you and I.

BRACKEN Yes.

BEAVERBROOK We have to save England from the bloody English, we Scots and Irish. Hah?

BRACKEN Indeed.

BEAVERBROOK Are you all right?

BRACKEN Yes. I'll see myself out.

BEAVERBROOK Brendan. (*Pause*) Your father was a remarkable man.

BRACKEN My father had the face of a condemned people.

BEAVERBROOK Brendan —

BRACKEN has gone.

(*Over the papers*) 'Mother's name: Hannah Ryan.' Pretty name, Hannah. (*Yell*) Arthur!

ARTHUR (*Off*) Yes, lord!

BEAVERBROOK Get some more papers, Arthur. More papers for my Deadman's Chest.

Lights down on BEAVERBROOK. Lights up on room. POPSIE stands in the middle of the room in the garb of the Women's Voluntary Service: long coat, armband, satchel over shoulder, tin-hat.

POPSIE (*Towards hidden BRACKEN who is off-stage*) That's not quite what I said. What I said was that you try too hard. That's all. It can be disconcerting to people. Can you hear me in there, Brendan? (*Almost to herself*) Very odd, really. It's rather as if something had been pushed out of shape and if one were only able to push it back into shape — Brendan!

BRACKEN   (*Off*) Yes. What is it?

POPSIE   Nothing. I simply said there is absolutely no reason why you should overstate yourself.

BRACKEN   Thank you.

POPSIE   Pig.

BRACKEN   Popsie!

POPSIE   Yes?

BRACKEN   Do you think that I am false?

She is so overwhelmed by this that she has to sit down.

(*Off*) Are you there?

POPSIE   Brendan, I think you're the most generous of persons.

BRACKEN   (*Off*) But do you think I'm false?

POPSIE   (*Near to tears*) No.

BRACKEN *comes on, briskly, in an overcoat and tin-hat.*

BRACKEN   There we are!

POPSIE   Where are you going?

BRACKEN   Up on the roof of the Admiralty, actually. I want to see the Hun arriving.

POPSIE   How ghastly!

BRACKEN   I have a rendezvous up there.

POPSIE   With whom, may I ask?

BRACKEN   With my great mechanical birds. Why not come with me?

POPSIE   I'm on duty now, you know. What I shall most remember of this war is the disgusting smell of tea-urns. (*Pause*) Are you really asking me to be with you, Brendan?

BRACKEN *has moved to the window and is peeping out. As he speaks she never even turns in his direction. She closes her eyes as if in discomfort.*

BRACKEN   Come here a moment, would you. Got to be

careful with the light. Look! Do you see that figure by the lamp post there? The one in the shoddy raincoat. That's him. That's my brother Peter. He will stay there until I have gone to bed. Where he sleeps I do not know. He's a criminal. Broke in here. Stole that Romney portrait of Burke from over the mantelpiece. Demanded a thousand pounds. I told him to bugger off. Look at him. Have you any conception, can you possibly understand what it is like? To be haunted by one's own brother dressed like a Soho pimp and with manners to boot. There are times, darling, when I truly fear that he may never go away from beneath the lamp post, there —

POPSIE Stop treating me like an audience!

> POPSIE *rushes out and off,* BRACKEN *calling after her. He then returns to his window. She has come downstage and across, hesitating, before she addresses the audience.*

I know you must think I've been frightful to him but really! I've been obliged to listen to stories about this brother for donkey's years. At different times this brother would appear to be high-up in the Admiralty, in charge of vast tea plantations in Ceylon while, at the same time, conducting a lucrative business in the City. He seems to dread the appearance of this brother on his doorstep. Like one of those messengers in an old play. Carrying a bundle of possessions, the swaddling clothes of a lost child. Perhaps, to keep him at bay, he is always talking about him. I will speak to the brother about it. Let me talk it over with the brother. People then smile at him. Behind his back, of course. Poor Brendan.

> *She pulls herself together and strides off to do her duty.* BRACKEN *watches through the curtains. He then steps out of the room and on to the rostrum,*

facing the audience, peering out. The ACTOR *comes forward in fire-warden gear, tin-hat, water-bucket. Stooped shoulders. As he does so, his attention, with* BRACKEN's, *is caught by the approaching drone of heavy bombers approaching London. He makes his way on to the rostrum behind* BRACKEN *from where they both look down on London from the roof of the Admiralty.*

WARDEN   Mr Bracken! Stand back from the edge there, sir.

BRACKEN   Righto, warden. (*Blitz up*) Look at them. Here they come. From beyond the Rhine. Out of the woods. Caesar saw them first. Painted bellies. Fire. And then the hordes.

WARDEN   Nothing to shout about, if you don't mind me saying so, sir.

BRACKEN   Mustn't give in to gloom, warden.

WARDEN   Not gloom, sir. Just what's before me eyes.

BRACKEN   (*Under breath*) Oh, my God, another roundhead.

WARDEN   Don't much like people up here in the bombing, sir, that's all.

BRACKEN   I am a member of the War Cabinet, warden.

WARDEN   Drinking champagne. Dancing. Not right, you know.

BRACKEN   Good God, man, I am to report to the PM and General Ismay.

WARDEN   Naked women in fancy clothes. Fellows in starched shirts that ought to be in the frontline. That's what I see up here, lolling about the place.

BRACKEN   (*Patriotically*) St Paul's still stands, warden. Indomitable.

WARDEN   Not much longer it won't, at this rate.

BRACKEN   This won't do, man! Haven't you seen our posters put up by the Ministry? '*Fight on the Home Front.*' '*Don't listen to Lizzie Longface and George Grumble.*' Got to keep your chin up, warden. I'm responsible for those posters, warden.

WARDEN   Bloody waste of time, if you ask me, sir. Besides we don't want to fall into the street, do we? Stones loose thereabouts. Jerry's handiwork.

BRACKEN Although I do agree with you that we have to watch for the enemy within.

WARDEN Only one enemy hereabouts, Mr Bracken, if you don't mind me saying so, sir.

BRACKEN Nonsense, man.

WARDEN Jerry up there. With the stick in his hands. Only enemy we've got, sir.

BRACKEN (*Very heated*) You've no idea, simply no idea — City filled with them! Ninnies! Twerps! Over there in Whitehall. Would sell the King for a pension. And don't forget our Lefties. Down in their cellars. Scribbling their manifestoes. Sabotaging our factories. Enemies! By god, man! Breaking into the Savoy with their filthy flags. All those Wogs and Frogs and Whatnots from every corner of Europe. Compared to that lot, warden, your Hun, your sausage-eater up there with his shaven head and his unspeakable language, why, my dear man, he's merely a schoolboy compared to that other shower —

WARDEN Poor blighters.

BRACKEN Who?

WARDEN Them down there. Doesn't matter who is who down there. You English, sir?

BRACKEN What do you mean by that, man?

WARDEN Just asking. No offence.

BRACKEN England is an idea, warden. Not just fifty thousand square miles of fertility on an island with some oddball Celts occupying mountains to the West and North.

WARDEN You're an educated man, sir.

BRACKEN Sedbergh, warden. I'm an old Sedbergian.

WARDEN Never heard of it. One of them public schools, is it?

He is rooting about with a contraption on the floor.

BRACKEN What's that, warden?

WARDEN It's only me primus, sir.

BRACKEN Primus! Primus! Lighting a primus in the middle

of an air-raid! This won't do, my man.

WARDEN Now look here, sir. You may be in charge down below. I'm in charge up here.

BRACKEN How very celestial of you.

WARDEN I know when Jerry's coming. When he's going. When he's gone.

    Blitz sounds down.

BRACKEN (*Shift. Profile*) I had a bit of bad news the other day, warden.

WARDEN Oh. What's that, then?

BRACKEN My brother. Died in action. The RAF. Died splendidly. One of 'Stuffy' Dowding's chaps. Life and soul of the mess. Shot down over the Isle of Wight. Hadn't a chance. Took down two Messerschmitts with him, though.

WARDEN Sorry to hear that, sir.

BRACKEN Terribly well liked at Marlborough. Rugger. The usual thing. Father would have been proud. Father was an admiral, y'know.

WARDEN Didn't know that, sir.

BRACKEN Family traditions are terribly important, warden.

WARDEN Funny that. My boy's in the RAF, too. What squadron did you say your brother was in, sir?

BRACKEN This is irregular, warden, most irregular. Lighting a primus in the middle of an air-raid.

WARDEN Who did you say your brother was with, Mr Bracken? What squadron is he in?

BRACKEN My brother — my brother is a traitor, warden.

WARDEN Not shot down?

BRACKEN Not shot down.

WARDEN Gone over to the other side, is he?

BRACKEN You might say that.

WARDEN Well well. Well well.

BRACKEN Where did your father live, warden?

WARDEN Eh?

BRACKEN Where did he live, your father?

WARDEN You mean me home, sir?

BRACKEN Yes.

WARDEN   Nelson Green. Baltic Street. Back of the Lavender Dock. We all worked the docks. Rotherhithe. My dad, his dad before him. Maybe his before him. Mostly casual. Not much left now, though. Wiped out. Down as far as Deptford.

> *A sudden, heavy explosion, all lights out and a single cry.* BRACKEN *in a flickering light.*

BRACKEN   (*Deep fear*) Daddy! Please — no! Mammy, Mammy! (*At first, faltering*) My father, my father who is, my father was — (*Low, strong Tipperary accent, boyish tone*) Me father was wan of the lads, so he was, wan of the hillside men. He took the oath. He was out in the tenants war of eighty-nine. (*Shift. Heavy adult voice*) Bejasus I was. I knew the treason prisoners of sixty-five. They were all great friends of yer father, so they were, the men that rotted away in Pentonville and Portland but bechrist their time will come again and when it does —

WARDEN   (*Voice out of the darkness*) Mr Bracken! Are you all right, sir?

BRACKEN   (*Irish accent, as before*) Come here, Peter, me son. Come here a minnit, me little man. You'll stand up for Ireland, won't you, boy, when you grow up, not like that brother of yours in the corner, Brendan-Brendy, the little scut, Mammy's pet, always whinging and bawling, four-eyes — (*English accent*) Leave me alone! Leave me alone!

WARDEN   (*With light*) You all right, sir?

BRACKEN   Is that you, warden? I cannot see. My glasses! Where are my glasses, man?

WARDEN   Here. Let me look about.

BRACKEN   I can't see. I'm blind.

WARDEN   Just the shock, sir. It'll pass in no time.

BRACKEN   For God's sake, I can't see!

WARDEN   Here's the specs.

BRACKEN   Broken, are they?

WARDEN   Right as rain, sir. Try them on.

BRACKEN What did — what was I saying a moment ago, warden? Just now.

WARDEN Something about your father, sir. I think. Couldn't quite get it.

BRACKEN I never knew my father, warden.

WARDEN No, sir.

BRACKEN He died when I was two years of age.

WARDEN Yes, sir.

BRACKEN They were once walked on, my glasses. I mean I once walked on them. The sound of terror, the glass. It's still black, warden.

WARDEN It's just the blast, sir. (*Sound of All Clear*) Raid's over. You want me to help you down below, sir?

BRACKEN What? No. No. Winston will wonder where I've been. Must go. Winston has been like a father to me, warden —

WARDEN Yes, sir.

BRACKEN Like a father.

BRACKEN *makes an unsteady exit.*

WARDEN (*After him*) What a lulu! Absolutely up in the bleeding belfry he is!

Light out on scene. Light up on BRACKEN *in his room, still wearing his overcoat. He fiddles with the wireless until he finds some music and sits, eyes closed. What happens is that the broadcast is interrupted by the voice of* JOYCE *calling to* BRACKEN *across the airwaves, at first the call signal: 'Germany calling! Germany calling!' Then the voice of* JOYCE, *at first spasmodically and then in full flow.* BRACKEN *is gradually alerted to it and his agitation increases with the presence of the voice. He switches off the wireless; the voice continues. He rushes off but the voice follows him so that we hear it at a distance as he stumbles about, beyond. When he comes back again the voice comes back with him and continues until he silences it.*

JOYCE (*On wireless*) We are one. You and I are one. Why
then, my friends, are we at war? The Germany
that I know and the England that I know are one,
two halves of the one, great, Northern European
culture and civilization. England is filled with our
friends. In every city, in every walk of life and
every class. How then have we been divided?
How have we been distracted from the common
enemy, the Bolshevik, the Mongolian hordes from
the East, waiting to descend upon Christendom.
The King of England was dethroned, not because
of an American lady but because he was a firm
friend of the Reich. A dummy was put in his
place, a puppet manipulated by Churchill who in
turn is manipulated by international Jewry —

BRACKEN *switches off the wireless and the voice
continues.*

I've watched you, Bracken, I've watched you for
years. You're just a gadabout, Bracken, bedazzled
by the finery in your master's house. I've watched
you, Bracken. I was at your elbow when you
lectured Von Ribbentrop in Lord Londonderry's
house in 1936 on Limoges china. Limoges china!
When serious offers were being made to forge the
alliance of the Teutonic peoples. I was beside you
and Mosley in 1935 when he told Churchill that
war with Germany would mean the destruction of
England and Germany with victory to red Russia
and the Jewish capitalists of America. And you,
Bracken! You could only offer a quip from Noël
Coward. I overheard you when you backed out of
going to Berlin with Lord Beaverbrook. The
Olympic games gave you the pip, you said. And
everyone went ho-ho. What a card! You're a
clown, Bracken. They know it. They know you're
just a performer. They like to see you perform,
don't you know that? It satisfies their taste in
comedy as a scale, a measurement, politics as

53

entertainment, entertainment as politics. In its decadence the imperial always transposes conquest into a circus. The more clownish Irish have always been willing to step into that ring. And you're the perfect clown because you believe that life is a matter of taste. That makes you entirely innocuous. They know that, Bracken. They know you do not matter.

BRACKEN *rushes off, out, the voice pursuing him.*

You're perspiring, Bracken. You're sweating. I can smell the swill in your stomach. Does it mean that, finally, the shell is cracking, Bracken? Are all the careful consonants out of control? What language will you speak now, my friend?

BRACKEN *backs out, the voice with him. After the first few lines the image of* JOYCE *appears on the video, black shirt, tie, black pants, and the voice speaks for the image.*

Surely you've thought about such things? You're an intelligent man. Educated by the Jesuits, back in Éire. As I was myself, indeed. We understand one another perfectly. The trouble with you, my friend, is that you have mistaken privilege for power. Privilege has nothing to do with power. Power is always rooted in reality. Ask your pal Beaverbrook. He would never make a mistake like that. I didn't make such a mistake. I have never been impressed by images. I went, instead, to the heart. I drank its blood. That is where passion is converted to power and power converted to rule. That is why I am hated and feared by you and your ilk, Bracken. Not because of my broadcasts. No. It is because I have pushed to the limits what you and your cronies would desire but could never push to the bitter end.

BRACKEN *stands before the hanging figures of Churchill, the King and Mosley and as he does so, the image and voice of* JOYCE *die out. Then he turns to a desk in the room and begins to busy himself with papers. He extracts an unfinished letter and makes some notes on it.*

BRACKEN (*Reading letter*) Dearest Mother, I have only now been able to reply to your letter. Of course I do understand the pain you feel as you reflect back upon your life. Of course I know how you suffered at the hands of that man, my father, that vicious person. I remember the scenes in Ardvullen House, Mother. I remember that barbaric man. How you lay in your own blood on the kitchen floor. How he broke the few pieces of china which you had brought with you as his bride into that house. I remember all these things, how could I ever forget! But, my dear, he is dead while you are living. To constantly remind oneself of past unhappiness is to be merely self-indulgent. You must put all that behind you as if it had never happened. Above all, one must utterly reject that which diminishes one, all that betrays one's higher instincts. One's sense of what it is to be civilized is what is important to one. There is nothing else.

A moment of reflection and, then, he leaves the room and comes down centre stage.

The ACTOR *and* ACTRESS *in their anonymous coats of the beginning come forward as well. The* ACTOR *reverses the portrait of Edmund Burke above the mantelpiece and flips the washing-line so that the figures of Churchill, the King and Mosley become Goebbels, Hitler and Mosley again. The* ACTRESS, *meanwhile, is helping* BRACKEN *to disrobe to* JOYCE: *beneath the overcoat there is the fascist black shirt and tie. Spectacles removed. Wig removed to close-cropped hair. A scar is exposed*

the full length of the face. JOYCE, *now ready,*
ascends the rostrum. Background marching sounds
for street corner political meeting. ACTOR *and*
ACTRESS *form a kind of audience but are eventually*
darkened out so that we are left, finally, with the
white face of JOYCE *in the darkness.*

JOYCE People of Manchester! In this year of the Lord,
nineteen hundred and thirty-three there is only
one question, my friends: Who is the Jew? Is he
your penny ha'penny shopkeeper on the corner?
Is he the Shylock moneylender, the usurer? Is he
the licene tailor of rainproofs with his throng of
Christian women and girls at the disposal of his
greasy fingers? Is he your Lord Israel and your Sir
Izzy in fur coats at the opera with their fat
consorts? Or is he the dark Russian in the International Club on Bury New Road preaching
Bolshevism? My friends, he is all these and more.
He is the common figure on our streets, he is the
secret agent. He is the parasite of our British
economy, the corrupter of our British heritage. He
is our evil otherness, the fault in our nature which
we must root out. My friends, the policy of the
British Union of Fascists, under our leader, Sir
Oswald Mosley, is simple, effective, humane. It is
that the island of Madagascar be appropriated by
the International Powers. That the island of
Madagascar be appointed the resting place of
all Jews. That all Jews be obliged to repair there
and that boats of the International Powers be
employed to patrol the waters about Madagascar
that no one escapes, ever again, off that island.
That, my friends, is the policy of the BUF. That is
our solution. For listen to this. Attend to this.
Assuredly if there be no Madagascar then there
will be Armageddon. The serpent of Judah is
encircling the globe and that encircling serpent is
seeking its own head. And when that head meets
its tail then this globe will be crushed by the Anti-

Christ of Judah. It is the serpent of history, my friends. It raises its head at seven points in history as outlined in the Protocols of Zion, the last, its apparition in St Petersburg in 1881. But the Bolshevik Jew of Russia and Capitalist Jew of Wall Street are alike in this. Each reaches out to the other. Each heralds the birth of the King born in Zion, Anti-Christ. Each is the instrument of the serpent. Each is awaiting that moment of cataclysm when the world will disintegrate, Russian Jew and American Jew, when that encircling serpent swallows its head, finally, in Jerusalem.

PART TWO

THE JOYCE PLAY: BERLIN

Before the lights go up: air-raid sounds in the distance which die out.
Then a battery of different radio stations over the air. Voices rise out
of static and snatches of music. The effect should be of someone
spinning a dial on the wireless.

WIRELESS (*Male and female voices*) Radio Caledonia calling,
Radio Caledonia calling — And now, here is
Radio Free Wales — Hello, *Worker's Challenge* on
the air — This is the New British Broadcasting
Station with transmitters in West London, East
Sussex and Kent. Tonight we will interview a
distinguished Knight of the Realm, who must, of
course, remain anonymous on why he is emi-
grating, with his family to Canada — Radio
Caledonia calling, Radio Caledonia calling. This
is Glasgow — This is Radio Free Wales, broadcasting from Aberystwyth: the time has come for
the valleys to rise up against the Saxon foe! —
And, now, here is *Worker's Challenge*, the voice of
the British proletariat, and here is Bert Jones who
will discuss the condition of the working class in
Britain today — Radio Caledonia calling, this is
Glasgow. Today we hear from Westminster that
supplies of coal and other essential goods are to be
cut back from Scotland — This is the BBC Home
Service and our microphone on the streets of
Britain today. Excuse me, madam, could we have
your views on what it is like to live on rationing

today? Well, I mean to say, how can a body live on what you get on the rations? It's ever so troublesome, that's what it is. What with all this bombing and no electric again yesterday I said to my friend Mavis, I said it's not bearable, that's what it is, not bearable —

Sound down. Lights up on the image of BRACKEN *on the screen.*

BRACKEN   Good evening. As Minister of Information in His Majesty's Government, it is my solemn duty to warn all loyal Britons against listening to these broadcasts. Do not be tricked by the Nazis and this chap Haw Haw. What Haw Haw is doing, you see, is sending out these broadcasts from Berlin and pretending that they're coming from inside Britain. No sensible Briton will be misled by this caddish deception. We know this gang in Berlin. We know their names. Our information and intelligence agents know this Haw Haw. He is an Irish traitor called William Joyce and well known to the police in this country. I want to make one thing perfectly clear. We in the Ministry of Information do not intend to stand idly by. We are going to get this traitor. He may go on for months more. But sooner or later the time will come and this man will have to face our British courts, our British law —

Image of BRACKEN *fades.* JOYCE *on the rostrum in a studio of the Rundfunkhaus, the broadcasting centre in Berlin, before a microphone and wearing a head-set. Panic-shouts off, stampeding feet in the building, bombs falling outside.* JOYCE *opens a drawer, removes a bottle of liquor and a glass and begins to drink, steadily. Sounds down and he stands, glass in hand, illuminated by flashes of light from outside.* ACTOR *and* ACTRESS *come on, to either side, in their neutral, narrator outfits.*

59

ACTRESS (*Narrator*) And, so, our scene shifts to Berlin —

ACTOR (*Narrator*) To the Rundfunkhaus, the radio centre of Dr Goebbels, the master propagandist of the Nazi Reich —

ACTRESS Where our hero sits.

ACTOR At the centre of the most extraordinary factory of voices ever assembled in the history of radio —

ACTRESS William Joyce, with his Germanic scar, acquired in a razor fight in Brixton —

ACTOR Our transposed Irishman, born in Brooklyn, New York City, but raised in the West of Ireland —

ACTRESS After a short period as an ultra-Englishman in England he ended up a naturalized German citizen of the Third Reich.

ACTOR To summarize: He was American but also Irish. He wanted to be English but had to settle on being German.

ACTRESS With his English-born wife, Margaret, known in German radio circles as Lady Haw Haw.

ACTOR Every night he brought into existence another England over the airwaves.

ACTRESS An England of articulate discontent —

ACTOR Is it any wonder that alone in his studio with a bottle of schnapps he could sit and feel a tremor of conquest?

ACTRESS England had once offered him a dream of supremacy. When it failed to deliver, it would have to be punished, with the punishment of an invented rebellion over the air.

ACTOR Down the corridor from him in the Rundfunkhaus were the other broadcasting stations of Dr Goebbels. There was the Indian Broadcasting Service, with real Indians, the Arab, the Scandinavian, the Irish, the Slav, the multiplying Tower of Babel of Dr Goebbels.

ACTRESS It was as if the whole world was about to be reinvented first, before its conquest by the Panzer divisions of the Wehrmacht.

ACTOR As if conquest were a relief from such clamorous discontent.

ACTRESS Is it any wonder that the Minister of Information was called in by the PM and asked to do something.

ACTOR (*Imitation Churchill*) Get Brenden Bracken on the phone. Something has to be done about this chap Haw Haw.

JOYCE We must become the voice of alternative possibilities. Find the right trigger. The spring. Take clocks, for instance. Clocks. Have you ever noticed how people become agitated when their clocks are interfered with? Hm? (*Announcement*) Listeners in Barnstead! Your town clock is fifteen minutes slow! Which, incidentally, it was. Result? Panic! (*Announcement*) Burghers of Cambridge, I promise you that the Luftwaffe will soon take care of your new Guildhall chronometer. Who the blazes told him about the clock? Or: you in Wolverhampton, go outside, go on, out you go. And look at the city clock. What do you see? Hm? Result? The release of the most potent subversion of all: the imagination of the people.

ACTRESS You see, a very curious thing was happening —

ACTOR As the listeners in Britain bent over the wireless every night twiddling the knobs towards Hamburg and Bremen, each listener became infected or, if you wish, inspired by the inventiveness of Mr Joyce —

JOYCE I said to them: To be effective propaganda has to be confirmation, at some level, of people's desires.

ACTRESS Each morning each person seemed to have a different story of what Lord Haw Haw had said the night before.

ACTOR Two people in the same room before the same wireless would report two different versions of what had been heard —

JOYCE What we say may be questionable. It must never be distasteful.

ACTRESS If William Joyce was re-inventing England, England was also re-inventing William Joyce.

ACTOR This is what is known as the Principle of Circularity.

ACTRESS Other students of the Imagination refer to it as the Double Cross Effect.

ACTOR It is endemic in situations of conflict between nations.

ACTRESS It frequently breaks out between writers and their readers.

ACTOR Who is telling whose story and to whom?

JOYCE (*Declaration of belief*) Every man has his secret desire to betray. It is intimately related to his desire for freedom. We simply need the key to unlock it.

ACTRESS (*Announcement*) Lord Haw Haw reveals the existence of a poker school in the back of a canteen in Ipswich!

ACTOR (*Announcement*) Lord Haw Haw warns the girls in an office in Fulham to stop sliding down the banisters! Or else!

ACTRESS Lord Haw Haw says he'll widen Orpington High Street and thereby stop a row on the Council.

ACTOR No wonder Mr Bracken was concerned.

ACTRESS As Minister of Information, that is —

ACTOR Information being his business, as it were —

ACTRESS And therefore misinformation as well, not to mention disinformation —

ACTOR It was as if a Ministry of Misinformation had been set up to counteract his Ministry of Information.

ACTRESS Absolute duplication —

ACTOR Or rather mis-duplication —

ACTRESS Intolerable.

ACTOR Insupportable.

ACTRESS Action simply had to be taken!

ACTOR And, at once!

They go off with a flourish. BRACKEN *appears, on the screen, behind a BBC microphone.*

BRACKEN Good evening. I regret to say that I must speak to you again tonight about Haw Haw, the Nazi broadcaster. Let us be perfectly frank about this. This is a free country. We may listen to what we like upon the wireless. This is England, not Germany, where people are put behind bars for listening to the BBC. That's not our way of doing things. We English are different. And are proud to be different. May I say this. The joke is over. It's about time to put a stop to this fellow once and for all. Above all, don't invent stories about Haw Haw just to impress your neighbours. Remember our slogan: Lies cost lives. Don't listen to Tittle-tattle Tom and Rumour Rodney. Put a notice on your wireless: This set doesn't listen to Haw Haw. Or something like that. Organize yourselves in groups, in the canteen, on the shop-floors: Loyalists for Britain! Loyalists against Haw Haw! And when you do hear a Haw Haw rumour report it to me at the Ministry. I will deal with it.

Lights out on the BRACKEN *image. Lights up on* JOYCE *on the rostrum in the semi-darkness before a window, out, toasting the bombing of Berlin. He is lit by flashes but otherwise there is silence. Centre rostrum: table, microphone, broadcasting studio.*

JOYCE 'The king who fights his people fights himself.
And they, thy knights, who loved me once, the stroke
That strikes them dead is as my death to me.'

He is drinking heavily throughout.

Papa always brought me with him to the Army Barracks in Galway. It was cold in the yard. Two officers were there. Is it quiet in the town, Joyce? Yes, sir. We depend upon men like you, Joyce, to keep the peace. Yes, sir. And who have we here? This is my son, sir. What age are you, boy? Fifteen, sir. And what is your name? William Brooke Joyce. Brooke? Brooke? That, surely, is not an Irish name, is it? His mother's name, sir. Her father was a medical doctor from Ulster. Ah! You are all Loyalists in your house, Joyce! Yes, sir. Well, carry on, Joyce. Keep up the good work. Then the lorries came in from patrol from the Clifden Road. Oughterard. Maam Cross. Moycullen. The Tans were drunk. But the officers only laughed. We shot some rabbits, one of the Tans shouted. Everyone laughed and I laughed. Then Papa went to the Paymaster's Office. Then I ran after the two officers. Just a moment, please! Yes? What is it? Ah, it is young William Joyce! Now, then, speak up. I want to serve, sir. You want to serve, do you? Yes, sir. The two officers looked at one another. And what can you do, boy? I know all the Sinn Féiners of the town, sir. The two officers looked at one another again. And, tell me, William Joyce, why do you wish to serve? I want to clean out the scum, sir. He wants to clean out the scum! Ha, ha! Well done, sir. Report to me in the morning, Joyce. Yes, sir. And the two officers saluted me. And I saluted them. And I turned away. And then. The last lorry of the patrol came into the yard.

Sudden shift. Leaps to table, seizes microphone, puts on head-set.

Hello-hello-hello. Is there anyone listening out there? Any chance of some juice, Fritz? They're all down in the bloody bomb shelter. I want to — Lord Haw Haw speaks to the besotted idealists of the earth, you know, all the starry-eyed believers in the improvement of the masses, God save the mark, as if homo sap could be dressed-up to be what he is not. Well, my friends, I've news for you. By the way, 's not bravado that I don't go down into the cellars. No. No, I have a rendezvous here with my great mechanical birds. I feed them, you see, from my window-sill. Also, there is the question of fastidiousness. Once our German friend hits the cellar during a raid he produces his sausage. The place reeks of garlic, compacted offal and broken wind. I often think there has to be significance, I mean, so much ingenuity, so much art in this race diverted into the making of sausages. (*Rise*) But back to my quixotic friends out there labouring to raise the filthy multitude to some level of decency and grace. You poor fools, can you not see that the human race is still at a primitive level of evolution? It is only our dreams that tell us what we might be if we were able, but able we are not, tied as we are to this ramshackle bag of a body. But I was about to say, my friends. There is no perfection without fire, no quickening without the burning lime, no redemption without ash. All you earnest believers in the perfectability of man attend! When the first great fire burned, the ice melted and the monkey stood upright in that incredible heat of the young sun. His brain expanded in its box. Words came from his mouth. Words refined the hanging jaw. And the nose melted into its human proportion. When the second great fire comes man will be burned again out of his imperfection and into the shape of his dreams.

He grabs the microphone, raises it aloft, then bangs it on the table and throws it to the floor. Drift away.

The last lorry came in from the patrol. A Crossley-Tender with wire-netting. Only the driver got out. He went and got a bucket of water. And threw it into the back. A great stream of blood came out. He got another bucket. And another. And another. So much blood that I thought that something was still bleeding in there.

Lights down on JOYCE. *Lights up on a drab sitting-*

room in wartime Berlin. The photograph of Hitler above the mantelpiece. The actor is ERICH: *plus-four tweeds, Norfolk jacket, Fair Isle pullover, good brogues. With his note-pad and pen he is taking English lessons from* JOYCE's *wife* MARGARET. *The* ACTRESS *wears a simple, floral dress: a scrubbed, tidy, pale English girl.*

ERICH (*Reading his essay*) 'Today is Monday. I go to my friend Jeremy in Kensington. Tomorrow will be Tuesday. I will go to shop in Fortnum and Mason's. I will buy my hamper for my picnic in the historic park of Windsor. Tomorrow and tomorrow will be Wednesday. I will go to Buckingham Palace to see the King.'

MARGARET No, Erich. That is incorrect. The day after will be Wednesday. Not tomorrow and tomorrow.

ERICH Tomorrow and tomorrow, no?

MARGARET No. I was quoting from Shakespeare when I used that phrase.

ERICH Ah, Shakespeare! To be or not to be, that is the question.

MARGARET Perhaps that is enough English lessons for today?

ERICH Please?

MARGARET I am tired, Erich.

ERICH I am tired, yes?

MARGARET You are tired?

ERICH No, no, no, no. It is good the lesson. You, Margaret. And William. You will teach me English and, then, I will speak English in England.

MARGARET Do you mean when England is occupied?

ERICH Certainly.

MARGARET I see.

ERICH The English peoples and the German peoples will join together. It is the hope of civilization. William believes it, does he not?

MARGARET Oh, yes. William believes that.

ERICH And you also, Margaret?

MARGARET I did not think there would be war, Erich.

ERICH But there is war.

MARGARET Don't misunderstand me, Erich. I believe one must be prepared to kill for what one believes.

ERICH Certainly.

MARGARET Are you prepared to kill, Erich?

ERICH (*Shrugs uncomfortably*) And William? William will kill, also?

MARGARET I don't really know, actually. So. I am the only one, then. How curious! It all seems so perfectly simple to me. William says I have a linear mind.

ERICH Linear? What is linear?

MARGARET Straight line. *Gerade linie.*

ERICH No, no, no. Not straight. (*He demonstrates curves and circles*) *Meine geliebte** Margaret is all circle.

He kisses her passionately and she responds, then pushes him away.

MARGARET You're very sweet, Erich. But not now, if you don't mind.

ERICH Sweet? Please explain.

MARGARET Sweet, warm. Passionate. Romantic.

ERICH Ah! Romantic. And William? William is romantic with my beloved Margaret?

MARGARET He's quite incredibly romantic but it doesn't come out that way. (*She suddenly bursts into tears*)

ERICH Please, Margaret. Is there something wrong? *Was habe ich dir getan?*** Oh, this is the end! Please, Margaret. I will say my poem. (*On one knee, declamation with gestures*)
'Sweetheart, do not love too long:
I loved long and long
And grew to be out of fashion
Like an old song.'

MARGARET *laughs at this. He holds her hands, shaking and kissing them when* WILLIAM JOYCE *walks in.*

BRACKEN Am I interrupting something? Do please continue. Do not let me —

*My beloved
**What have I done to you?

MARGARET Our lesson has ended.

JOYCE So I see.

ERICH Your wonderful poet, Herr Joyce. The beauty of England. Moonlight and olden dances. Avalon and Lancelot and others also of the joyous island.

MARGARET Erich —

JOYCE To whom are you referring, nay, I ask, which poet are you extemporizing with such *élan*?

ERICH Yeets.

JOYCE Keats?

ERICH No, no, no, no. Yeets. I will arise and go now and go to Inish-free.

JOYCE Ah, Yeats. W. B. Yeats.

ERICH Certainly.

JOYCE My dear fellow, Yeats isn't English.

ERICH No?

JOYCE No. Yeats is Irish. He is writing about Ireland. Different place, alas.

MARGARET Don't listen to him, Erich.

JOYCE So, you wish to study English literature, Erich?

ERICH Certainly.

MARGARET You are mocking Erich.

JOYCE Am I mocking Erich? I am not mocking Erich. I would never dream of mocking Erich.

ERICH (*To* MARGARET) Forgive me, Margaret, I must go. Thank you for the wonderful lesson. We will have a lesson next week? Thank you. Yes. (*Turning to* JOYCE *with a bow*) *Mein Herr!*

Exit ERICH.

MARGARET Shall I prepare some food?

JOYCE No, thank you very much.

MARGARET I think you've been beastly to him.

JOYCE Who? What? Hm?

MARGARET Please, William, don't —

JOYCE What? What? What?

MARGARET Stop it! Stop it! I can't abide your mockery now. It's so utterly out of place, so crude, so inappropriate to Erich —

JOYCE I'm worried, Margaret. Truly. I'm worried about your judgement. I really am. This ridiculous buffoon in his Harris tweeds —

MARGARET Erich is a friend.

JOYCE Erich is an ass.

MARGARET Don't you realize — everyone, every place, everyone, finally, at some point fails to measure up in your estimation — your high standard —

JOYCE If you wish to defend that bumbling fruit —

MARGARET Why, William? That's what I want to know?

JOYCE He, actually, really does believe, you know that he is in possession of the mysteries of English poetry, that clown, master of the English lyric!

MARGARET Will you ever be satisfied, William? Ever?

JOYCE That pumped-up, would-be *Gauleiter* of the British Museum —

MARGARET Every night I sit in this miserable room waiting for you to return while you sit drinking in the Kaiserhof with those American newspapermen. It is intolerable!

JOYCE I am surprised at you, Margaret. You've forgotten, Margaret. Have you forgotten? All those promises, those undertakings? All those talks we've had down the years. Don't you remember? How we dreamed of working together towards the one goal?

MARGARET Yes. Absolutely.

JOYCE The one cause.

MARGARET I remember that we had an understanding William. Didn't we? That each should be free. No vulgar little middle-class inhibitions and restrictions. Your own words, William. Man and woman in absolute, natural freedom. Or have I imagined it?

JOYCE Yes, yes. The rooting out of everything that was common and shabby and second-rate —

MARGARET Why, Erich isn't at all like that!

JOYCE Erich! Erich? Erich is irrelevant. It is you, Margaret, we're talking about. We're talking about you.

MARGARET This is preposterous!

JOYCE Maybe you'd prefer to go back to Manchester? Hm? Back to East Lancaster Fabrics? Would you? Would you, Margaret? And marry that nice GP? Hm? Settle down with an Austin and a terrier in Whitefield. Is that what you really want, Margaret? Perhaps you regret everything you've done with me? Do you?

MARGARET My dear William Joyce, anything I have done I have done out of my own will, I assure you. You know you're being quite offensive. I intend to ignore it.

JOYCE Don't you ignore it, Margaret.

MARGARET Why are you doing this? Now? At this time?

JOYCE I do it because I intend to shake you out of this suburban mush, this wallow of mediocrity into which you periodically sink —

MARGARET No!

JOYCE Yes, Margaret.

MARGARET I don't need your bullying, thank you.

JOYCE Oh but you do. You need constant pressure, Margaret, to remain steadfast.

MARGARET No, I do not. I have sacrificed everything to be here. There is no going back.

JOYCE Yes, but what about the bad days, Margaret? Those days, those hours when you buckle, you wilt —

MARGARET No!

JOYCE Yes, Margaret. And afterwards you thank me for holding tight. Thank you for holding on, William. Then you kiss my hands. And I lift you up.

MARGARET (*Low*) Yes.

JOYCE You do admit to that, don't you, Margaret?

MARGARET Yes.

JOYCE And then I take you to me.

MARGARET (*Very low*) Yes.

JOYCE And we become one.

MARGARET (*Cry*) I help you, too!

JOYCE Of course.

MARGARET Often —

JOYCE I could never have survived without you.

MARGARET When you speak of giving in —

70

JOYCE Yes.

MARGARET Your depressions —

JOYCE I know, I know.

MARGARET When you take the razor ready to slash yourself, it is I who stop you, William.

JOYCE Yes.

MARGARET When you're ready to surrender, it is I who say no. When you talk of moving on, as if, good heavens, there could be anywhere left in the world for us to move to — I say stop, stop, stop, no more, this is it, this is our chosen ground, this is where we must stand because everything has led to this like a straight line across a map.

JOYCE Yes.

MARGARET And your howling at night, William, when you howl like that against the waste of it all it is I who take you in my arms.

She embraces him, holds him.

JOYCE I know.

MARGARET Then why do you subject me to this?

JOYCE We must bite into our love every day.

MARGARET I don't need to do that, William.

JOYCE To be alive.

MARGARET (*Kissing him*) It's really so very much more simple than that, dear, if you would allow it to be.

JOYCE Against all contamination.

MARGARET Dear William, I do believe you were jealous? Were you?

JOYCE It is our bond.

MARGARET Were you? Were you jealous?

JOYCE What? What?

MARGARET Of Erich? Jealous?

JOYCE I would never insult you by associating you with that stuffed bag of wind, that obscenity — Besides, Margaret, from now on we must contain ourselves, draw ourselves into dignity. Are you listening, Margaret?

MARGARET Pardon?

JOYCE Germany is defeated. It is only a matter of time. We will continue as before. But our knowledge must make us resolute. We must be circumspect. We must build our own citadel. You are not listening, Margaret!

MARGARET Sorry, no. I mean I can't attend to one of your lectures, William, not now at any rate.

JOYCE This is not one of my lectures!

MARGARET Yes, well, it's extremely difficult.

JOYCE Do you not know how we must steel ourselves?

MARGARET I didn't intend to tell you this but you've left me little choice.

JOYCE What? What?

MARGARET If you must know, Erich and I have been intimate.

JOYCE Intimate?

MARGARET Yes, intimate.

JOYCE You what?

MARGARET It was simply the most natural expression of what we felt for one another. He was such a dear and I, well, I was lonely. You might say that we came together playing out some impossible but perfectly delightful romance. It was nothing more than that, really.

He slaps her so that she sinks to the floor. He immediately goes to her in a state of guilty recriminations.

JOYCE Oh, Margaret, I'm sorry, I'm sorry, sorry, sorry. I never meant — have I hurt you, oh, please forgive me, Margaret, please —

MARGARET It's all right, William. Help me up, would you —

JOYCE I'm a thug, that's all, a vicious — I love you —

MARGARET Yes, I know.

JOYCE I want you. I want you now, Margaret. Let us make love, Margaret, now, please make love immediately.

He is trying to kiss her so that she has to push him away.

MARGARET For heaven's sake, William, do you mind!

JOYCE What have I done? What did I do wrong? How did I fail you? You weren't happy with me. Was that it? Obviously I failed you. I can understand that. But you must say it to me. Say it now, Margaret, say how I failed you. Did I fail you? What did I do? Was it something in our lives together? Why didn't you tell me?

MARGARET Please, William —

JOYCE Some way that I failed? I didn't know. I cannot understand it. Explain it to me. Was it sexual? Did I fail you sexually? For you to go and — was it that? You never indicated that. You never suggested you were unhappy in that way.

MARGARET It's absolutely nothing like that!

JOYCE Then why, why, why, why, why —

MARGARET It is so perfectly simple, so ordinary!

JOYCE You're a filthy cunt, you know that? You're just a whore. How many more have there been? Answer me. Acting the madam. I see it now. A vile bitch in heat allowing that dirty kraut to put his thing into you. What else did you do with him, hm? You enjoyed it, didn't you, foul, dirty bitch. I can smell him off you, you know that —

MARGARET There is nothing wrong! There is nothing wrong!

JOYCE Whore!

MARGARET Don't, William, please, don't you see how you're degrading yourself?

JOYCE It is the betrayal, the betrayal —

MARGARET Nonsense — How could I have betrayed you if we were both free? Both meeting as absolutely independent, mature, adult persons? For heaven's sake, William, we've put all that bourgeois rubbish behind us. I could never be promiscuous. But neither is my sexuality the property of you or anyone else. Our love transcends all that, William — How could one possibly betray something which simply doesn't control one?

JOYCE You are no longer my Margaret.

MARGARET William, you must simply listen to what I say.

JOYCE I should beat the shit out of you —

MARGARET I am going to repeat your own words to you, William —

JOYCE Leave me alone —

MARGARET No, William, you must listen. I insist that you recover yourself, through yourself, through your own words. We must turn our violence into energy. That's what you said. We must use that energy to master the world about us. Don't you remember? Your words, William Joyce. Personal violence is waste. Violence controlled and directed is power. Power! Power!

JOYCE I can't go on.

MARGARET Of course you can go on. You must go on.

JOYCE (*Sudden switch-on*) But I must have done something. What did I do? What was it? Was it sex? Was it neglect? Of course I neglected you —

MARGARET Stop it, William. At once —

JOYCE I did stay out late. I needed to, you see, to relax, to come back from the broadcasts, to unwind. Don't you understand that? Not neglect: no. Failure. Did I fail? How did I fail?

MARGARET William!

JOYCE Perhaps if I were to — By God, I'll get that idiot. Of course. I see it plainly. You've made a fool of me. I've indulged you. If only I had — You filthy fucking bitch, wallowing in that sty with that gross fucker —

MARGARET *rushes out. He follows and his voice is heard as the lights come down.*

You won't get away with this, do you hear? Answer me or by Christ I will — You can't run away, you can't escape —

Lights up: MARGARET *is sitting in the room.* JOYCE *is walking about. Both are dishevelled, wasted. He talks but it is as if he no longer needs a listener. She is utterly spent.*

JOYCE   What have I done? What did I do wrong? How did
         I fail you? You weren't happy with me. Was that
         it? Obviously I failed you. I can understand that.
         But you must say it to me. Say it now, Margaret.
         Say how I failed you. Did I fail you? What did I do?
MARGARET (*Quietly, after endless repetition*) William, stop.
         Please stop. You've talked non-stop for twenty-
         four hours. We haven't slept. We haven't eaten.
         We simply cannot go on like this. You must stop
         talking.
JOYCE   What was it? I don't understand. Try to explain to
         me.
MARGARET William!

> *She rushes out. He continues to sit there, mumbling
> down into silence. She comes down to audience.*

Finally, it stopped. That sickening spill of words.
I thought I should never hear that voice stop. But
it did. It was like an engine running down. There
was always some gap between what he said and
what he really felt. When that gap widened all that
was left to him was speech. When he stopped
talking there was silence for weeks. Then he said
we would be divorced. I said, don't be ridiculous.
But he said: we must be divorced. Very well, I
said, if that is what you want. We went to court. I
will never forget that room: 34A Zivilkammer.

> JOYCE *comes down and joins her.*

I had difficulty understanding the German.
JOYCE   Do you, William Joyce, petition for divorce from
         Margaret Joyce, on the grounds of infidelity?
         (*Pause*) I do.
MARGARET Do you, Margaret Joyce, counter-petition for
         divorce from William Joyce, on the grounds of
         cruelty and neglect? (*Pause*) I do.
JOYCE   Do you, William Joyce, contest the charges of the
         other party? (*Pause*) I do not.

MARGARET Do you, Margaret Joyce, contest the charges of the other party? (*Pause*) I do not.

JOYCE And do you, Margaret Joyce, apply for the payment of alimony?

MARGARET I am sorry. My German is poor. I do not understand the question.

JOYCE Explain the question to the woman.

MARGARET No. No. I am perfectly able to support myself.

JOYCE Then this divorce is granted with the parties to pay their own costs.

They turn and face one another for a few seconds. Then they collapse, tearfully into one another's arms, crying one another's names.

JOYCE We will get married again.

MARGARET Not today, if you don't mind.

JOYCE I will never leave you.

MARGARET I don't intend to allow you.

JOYCE Let us go home.

MARGARET Yes.

They re-enter the apartment together, she tense, he in a daze.

William —

JOYCE Yes —

MARGARET I have to tell you.

JOYCE Yes?

MARGARET Erich is waiting —

JOYCE I see.

MARGARET To say goodbye.

JOYCE Goodbye?

MARGARET Yes. He is going to the Eastern Front. (JOYCE *gives a wild whoop of laughter*) Please, William, do not mock.

JOYCE The Third Reich is in serious trouble.

MARGARET Older men and boys have been called up.

JOYCE I see.

ERICH makes his entrance. The effect should be striking, not least on JOYCE. ERICH is in the officer's uniform of the Waffen SS. It is as if the uniform has changed the man, his carriage, status, his power. He brings with him something of the immense armour of German militarism.

ERICH (*Bow*) Margaret. Herr Joyce. *Ich gehe jetzt on die Front und kampfe für Volk und Vaterland.* ['I go now to the front to fight for nation and fatherland.']
MARGARET Oh, Erich.
ERICH I go to fight the Bolshevik, Herr Joyce.
MARGARET But, Erich, you are too old.
ERICH Old? Old? What is this old? Now I must go.

He takes MARGARET's hand and kisses it.

'*Ein Blick von dir, ein Wort mehr unterhalt, als alle Weisheit dieser Welt*, Margaret.' ['A glance from you, a word pleases more than all the wisdom of this world, Margaret.'] Goethe's *Faust*.
JOYCE No more English poetry, Erich? Only German poetry now?
ERICH Certainly, Herr Joyce. No English poetry. German poetry now.

He turns to JOYCE, walks towards him and gives the Nazi salute.

Heil Hitler!

ERICH's salute should have the effect of slowly forcing JOYCE's arm up, as if by the pressure of power. When ERICH's arm drops, so does JOYCE's. ERICH clicks his heels and departs.
   The lights come down on the noise of bombing and war sounds which reach a crescendo and then, suddenly, silence. The image of BRACKEN appears on the screen.

BRACKEN   The war is over. But our work at the Ministry of Information has not ended. It must continue until the whole Nazi machine is dismantled, until Nazi propaganda is silenced forever. There is a category of war criminal that is of special interest to our Ministry and to me as Minister of Information. I refer to the traitor broadcasters and in particular to the arch traitor, William Joyce. No stone must be left unturned, no loophole left open in the pursuit of these rats, these perverts. While these renegades continue to live in freedom our British self-respect, indeed our very British identity, is threatened. They cast a shadow over our very existence. Haw Haw must be taken. The full force of British justice must be executed upon this man.

As the image fades, lights up on MARGARET *and* JOYCE *dismantling their apartment and frantically packing, flashes of explosions lighting them as they work. Bombing and approaching war sounds.* JOYCE *and* MARGARET *hurriedly assemble suitcases and bundles and put on trench-coats. They come forward.*

JOYCE   Have we got all our papers?
MARGARET   Of course we do.

They take a rest. She sits on a suitcase.

(*To audience*) I watched William all the time. He had spoken so often of how he would die that I thought — I have always had contempt for suicide.
JOYCE   (*To audience*) She was magnificent. I watched her to see if she would crack. It was essential that she did not crack. I had already written our future, you see, and it was imperative that we follow the lines to the bitter end.
MARGARET   First, we were all moved to the Dutch border. The

English were only twenty-five miles away. Puffs of smoke hung over the horizon and everywhere there was a sudden, great silence. Then back to Bremen. To Hamburg.

JOYCE In Hamburg I delivered my last broadcast.

MARGARET It was unreal. Suddenly there was no more rationing. Everyone had food and drink. And everywhere this silence.

JOYCE I warned England. I said that without Germany, the British Empire would disappear within a decade. I said the Russian Empire already extended from Poland to the Black Sea, from Moscow to the suburbs of Berlin. I said that England would be impoverished. Reduced to selling its treasure to Americans. Is this what this war was fought for?

MARGARET He was incoherent. Once word came of the suicides of Hitler and Goebbels he drank, steadily, day and night. We were told to say that Hitler had died at a street barricade. I insisted upon telling everyone that he had taken his own life.

JOYCE I wanted Margaret to be with me. I wanted so desperately that she be beside me to the end.

MARGARET I did not want William to die.

JOYCE (*Rise*) I said that England had been denied her place in the foundry of human progress, forging the new Adam, *Novus homo* of the new millennium —

MARGARET Then one morning as papers were burned by the Propaganda Ministry and false papers handed out — that strange collection of races all yelling out different choices of new nationalities — word came on the telephone, still miraculously working, from Berlin —

JOYCE England was ruined by a gang. The American Jew-lover Churchill and his cronies, effete degenerates like Bracken, monied gangsters like Beaverbrook.

MARGARET It said we were to be taken by U-boat to a spot on the west coast of Ireland.

JOYCE I refuse to go there! I will not hear of it! I will not be condemned to a living death.

MARGARET It was then that I realized that I, too, had given myself to death. I mean I had always thought of our love as being for the sake of life. Now I knew it was for the sake of death. And, do you know, this made absolutely no difference to my love for him.

JOYCE I loved her so much that I had to know where she was every hour of every day.

MARGARET We left the towns with what we could carry and joined the lines of people crossing the quiet countryside, going nowhere. When the first truckloads of English soldiers came through he started — he began his dangerous, silly game —

JOYCE (*Yell*) You all right, mate? Anyone there from Manchester?

MARGARET Again and again he would yell out, with that wild laugh of his, even at English soldiers standing right beside him.

JOYCE I say, officer, when is the next bus to Berlin?

MARGARET He called it his Irish roulette. And, do you know, I believe he was pretty disappointed when his voice was not recognised. Did he know what he was doing?

JOYCE I knew exactly what I was doing. I was going to the village of Küpfermühle above Wasserleben.

MARGARET There were times, as I watched him, that I felt he had already been taken away from me.

JOYCE And when we reached Küpfermühle it was May and the sun was shining.

MARGARET There was this English widow living in the village since 1912. She could hardly speak English any more. She took us in.

JOYCE Sometimes I lay on the ground for hours in the sunshine contemplating the buds on the birch trees.

MARGARET She used to invite English soldiers on duty in the village to tea. Nice boys from Bradford and Leeds. They gave us the *Daily Mirror*. They talked about going home. They never questioned who this couple might be, who called themselves Herr and Frau Hansen.

JOYCE Sometimes I went for walks in the woods above Wasserleben.

They stand and face one another. She fusses with his coat. They kiss.

MARGARET Do you have your papers?

JOYCE (*Clicking heels, bow*) Fritz Hansen, teacher of English.

MARGARET Is it possible that I may never see you again?

JOYCE It is possible.

MARGARET I believe that one day it will all begin again.

JOYCE I believe so, too.

MARGARET I have been blessed, William, to have been loved by you.

They embrace. He steps away from her and she sits on the suitcase with her back to him.

JOYCE (*To audience*) I walked out through Wasserleben and into the woods. I left behind the smell of insufficient food, the strained faces and that impossible hiatus between conquest and punishment. And I knew precisely what was waiting for me in that clearing in the woods. I walked, quickly, now, because all that remained was to be exemplary. The two English officers were ahead of me and walking through the clearing. I almost ran after them. Just a moment, please! Yes? What is it? Speak up. I want to serve, sir. What? I want to serve. The two officers looked at one another. They seemed to be remembering, to be reminding one another of something. You wouldn't, by any chance, you wouldn't be William Joyce, would you? I said I am — and I raised my hand towards the pocket where my forged papers were. Fritz Hansen, teacher of English. He had pulled the revolver quickly and shot all in the one movement. Because I had turned slightly the bullet entered and passed through my right thigh and entered and passed my left thigh making, in all, four wounds. The man who shot me was called Perry. But that was not his real name. All Jews serving in the British Army in Germany were advised to change their names. I had been shot by a Jew pretending to be a Briton in the woods above Wasserleben.

He removes the trench-coat. MARGARET *opens a suitcase and puts in the trench-coat, having taken out a standard, 1940s prison jacket.* JOYCE *puts on the jacket and steps on to the rostrum.* MARGARET *watches him a moment. Then she gathers the bundles and suitcases and, heavily laden, goes off. Lights on the image of* BRACKEN *on the screen.*

BRACKEN We have finally silenced Haw Haw. Throughout his trial he scarcely spoke a word. That voice which had taunted us throughout the long nights of the war, that ridiculous accent, was gone. Perhaps he was overwhelmed by the majesty of our British law? The carved, royal standard of the courtroom? The sword of justice in its jewelled scabbard above the judge's chair? Or maybe words were only available to him when he lied and threatened us on the wireless? I saw this man once. I heard him speak at one of Mosley's meetings before the war. I heard him turn speech into a deadly weapon of hate and destruction. There were other misguided Britons before the war, Nazi-sympathizers and appeasers. But most of those people rallied to the call of Mr Churchill when the time came. This man was different. He tried to turn Britain against itself. He was as much our enemy as all the saboteurs, the spies and fifth columnists who tried to bomb our cities and factories during the war. There can be no peace while a man like this is allowed to live.

The actress as a LADY JOURNALIST *comes forward to the side of the rostrum. She addresses herself to* JOYCE *as if he were a specimen to illustrate her points. She is dressed in elegant '30s clothes with, perhaps, a hat and large feather.*

JOURNALIST I covered the treason trial of William Joyce. I was in the Old Bailey in September 1945 when he was condemned to be hanged. Here was a man driven by an inappropriate reverence for the country he had betrayed. He had spoken, at length, and even in the act of treason itself, about his British heritage, his love of the Union Jack, of the throne, of the Empire, but to civilized people of this country his extravagance was merely vulgar. When he was a demagogue on our streets his few followers were misfits and the misled. But it is a hallmark of British civilization that it sheds coarse extravagance. Its power is in its discrimination, its grace is in its refinement of what in other cultures become crude images. William Joyce would never know anything of this. Those who saw him in the dock were struck by his undernourishment, the product of generations of peasant breeding. He did have the cockiness of your typical Donnybrook Irishman but it fitted uneasily with the acquired, clicking heels and the silly teutonic bow. William Joyce was condemned out of an inexplicable desire which could only be satisfied by his own destruction. In his trial, the judge found that he had never been a British citizen at all. He was an alien. His British passport was false. But the symbol is greater than the fact. Once he carried that passport, however spurious, William Joyce had put himself beneath the King's protection and therefore could be judged a traitor to the King. His act was at once loyal and disloyal and as such was both contradictory and repugnant. No man can decide for himself what it is to be loyal to the British Crown. It is decided for him. So, William Joyce was condemned to death. And after that it was but a matter of waiting for the white card to be pasted on the door of Wandsworth Prison.

> *She sits and waits. Sound of clanging doors and footsteps on corridors.*
> BEAVERBROOK *steps up on the rostrum and into* JOYCE's *cell.* BEAVERBROOK *takes notes throughout.*

BEAVERBROOK I am Max Aitken.

JOYCE I know who you are. You are Lord Beaverbrook.

BEAVERBROOK It was good of you to see me.

JOYCE I was curious. Why should you want to see me, Lord Beaverbrook, since your newspapers howl for my blood along with the Jew-boars and the Jew-sows of this condemned city?

BEAVERBROOK I am interested in the profound fidelities produced by treason.

JOYCE During my appeal in the Lords I sat in the becoroneted chair in the Royal Robing Room and looked out on the river and Lambeth Bridge. As Conrad said, What greatness had not floated on the ebb of that river! And I thought it was ironical to consider that I had more Norman blood in my veins than many of those titled duds waiting outside for the kill.

BEAVERBROOK I have always felt that there was something screwball about this emphasis on nationality.

JOYCE Absolutely! What does some absurd, adjectival, geographical method of denoting origin actually mean? That one was sired in this hole or that hole. I am only interested in the future of the human race.

BEAVERBROOK I have a friend. I once nearly lost his friendship by exploring his birthplace.

JOYCE What is his name?

84

BEAVERBROOK Brendan Bracken.

JOYCE I have never met him.

BEAVERBROOK Do you find prison very disagreeable?

JOYCE On the contrary. Apart from my Jesuit school in Galway, prison is the only place in which I have seen psychology applied, consistently and sensibly, in the running of an institution.

BEAVERBROOK I interviewed Rudolf Hess, too, you know, when he landed in Scotland.

JOYCE The German's reputation for psychology is grossly over-rated. That quack Freud and his stinking mind. I believe in Gestalt. I believe in the survival of electro-magnetic systems. Another medium. Beyond — Margaret —

BEAVERBROOK And what are your fidelities now, Mr Joyce?

JOYCE I face my Lord Jesus purged of all impurities.

BEAVERBROOK I know one thing, for sure. Betrayal produces its own fidelities. You betray the small when you give yourself to the great. That is what is known as progress. But what really grabs me is the point at which betrayal opens the abyss, where it becomes so intolerable that the betrayer has to be hunted down and destroyed.

JOYCE Can we not get beyond this fiddle-faddle?

BEAVERBROOK It's as if treason creates a reflection of what is betrayed — so intolerable that it has to be destroyed — a kind of terrifying mirror or something —

JOYCE I am British.

BEAVERBROOK Oh, anyone can be British. Doesn't matter who you are, where you come from, what the colour of your skin is. All you need is a modest command of the language and a total commitment to a handful of symbols, some of which are pretty ludicrous. But they work. Would it surprise you, Mr Joyce, if I told you that you nearly got off?

JOYCE What is this questioning?

BEAVERBROOK It's true —

JOYCE I've passed beyond concern for my fate on this earth.

BEAVERBROOK Sure. I see that.

JOYCE (*Fury*) Getting off! Getting off! Oh, my God. (*Pause. Cry*) Where is Margaret?

BEAVERBROOK It's true, nevertheless. I heard it from the Lord Chancellor himself. Two lords voted for acquittal. Two for the death penalty.

JOYCE And my Lord Chancellor decided?

BEAVERBROOK Well, they persuaded Lord Macmillan to switch his vote as a matter of fact. So there were now three lords for the death penalty, one for acquittal. Much better. Then the Lord Chancellor voted for the death penalty. Although he knew perfectly well that it was bad law.

JOYCE I see.

BEAVERBROOK Thought you might be interested. It's politics, I'm afraid. Politics is a very simple-minded business, Mr Joyce, at its most effective.

JOYCE You make it sound like a trivial accident, my friend.

BEAVERBROOK Certainly not.

JOYCE I have given my life that men may rise above their common weakness.

BEAVERBROOK Oh, I acknowledge that, yes.

JOYCE I have shown them how to master nature.

BEAVERBROOK Well — yes. I'm afraid that may be why we have to hang you, Mr Joyce.

JOYCE What is this man talking about?

BEAVERBROOK Any man who thinks he can master nature is a threat to British civilization. The basis of our civilization, Mr Joyce, is common sense.

JOYCE There are times when I no longer see. When there is no light. Then I call to Margaret.

BEAVERBROOK Mr Joyce —

JOYCE I will not be cast off, do you hear!

BEAVERBROOK Well, it's odd. I mean, have you ever thought, it may be some consolation to you, indeed, at this terrible time — I mean, passport or no passport, Britain has acknowledged you British by deciding to execute you for treason. Identity can be a fiction, Mr Joyce, and be no less satisfactory on that account.

JOYCE I have helped to shape things —

BEAVERBROOK I couldn't agree more. Indeed, that's why I'm here. I am always fascinated by the select, those to whom history has given a choice —

JOYCE And now, God my Father, I will rest in Thee.

BEAVERBROOK I met Hitler, too, you know. Tell me. What did you think of Hitler?

JOYCE I never saw Hitler.

BEAVERBROOK And Goebbels? What about Goebbels?

JOYCE I never met Goebbels.

BEAVERBROOK Yeah — well, that's fantastic. That's a whopper!

JOYCE Are you copying down all of this?

BEAVERBROOK Sure. I'm a journalist. I chase stories.

JOYCE Like all journalists you have an exaggerated sense of the power of words.

BEAVERBROOK My friend, I've changed the government in this country through my printed words. It depends on the ability to use words to create power.

JOYCE Maybe, indeed.

BEAVERBROOK So, you've found religion, have you?

JOYCE Do not patronize me or my faith.

BEAVERBROOK I do not patronize you. In my house, on the lawn in Stornoway House there is a life-sized crucifix. I can see it as I sit at my dining-room table.

JOYCE But you're eating your dinner at the same time are you not? (BEAVERBROOK *chuckles at this*) Oh, my Christ Jesus, there is no more time! Why did Hess fly to Scotland?

BEAVERBROOK He told me he wished to see his friend the Duke of Hamilton. Do you think he might be nuts?

JOYCE The fools, the fools! If they had only listened to what we said in 1936.

BEAVERBROOK Do you mean Mosley? Or the Nazis?

JOYCE Mosley was the creation of a group of upper-class English whores who needed leather. Why are you asking me these things? It does not matter. Do you think this war was fought for some piddling sentimentality out of Rupert Brooke? This war was fought and lost on behalf of the species.

BEAVERBROOK Hess said a peculiar bloody thing. He said he saw a vision of Armageddon from his aeroplane.

JOYCE Perhaps he was flying into freedom before he crashed. His freedom. Freedom is just beyond what is, it is the perfection of our desires and therefore cannot be achieved in the present dimension.

BEAVERBROOK I see you've been reading, Mr Joyce. What are you reading?

JOYCE Thomas à Kempis.

BEAVERBROOK I see.

JOYCE I would prefer to be alone now.

BEAVERBROOK Yes. OK. OK by me.

JOYCE Let *me* ask *you* some questions, Lord Beaverbrook.

BEAVERBROOK Shoot.

JOYCE Do you think this war has destroyed the British Empire?

BEAVERBROOK Yes.

JOYCE And did you know that at the beginning of the war?

BEAVERBROOK Yes.

JOYCE And yet you, the great imperialist, gave everything to the war effort?

BEAVERBROOK Sure.

JOYCE I don't understand.

BEAVERBROOK That's why you're where you are now, Mr Joyce, and why I am somewhere else. (JOYCE *laughs at this*) I never mistake rigidity for authority, Mr Joyce.

JOYCE And am I to appear in the *Daily Express*, Lord Beaverbrook?

BEAVERBROOK No, no, no. Those are papers for my Deadman's Chest, Mr Joyce.

JOYCE And what is that?

BEAVERBROOK A kind of box, Mr. Joyce. Posterity, Mr Joyce. Yeah, posterity.

BEAVERBROOK *goes off and leaves* JOYCE *alone in the light. On the video* BRACKEN *appears as if behind bars or a grille of iron. The mood is one of reverie.*

JOYCE You should not have come here.
BRACKEN I had to come.
JOYCE Why?
BRACKEN Because I am searching for my brother.
JOYCE Your brother isn't here.
BRACKEN I have searched everywhere else.
JOYCE What does he look like, your brother?
BRACKEN My brother has the face of a condemned people.
JOYCE I have seen many faces in here that look like that.
BRACKEN I searched the streets.
JOYCE Have you looked in all the places of detention?
BRACKEN I have only begun the search.
JOYCE Well, then, why not come back again, tomorrow?

JOYCE *comes alert, with uptilted face. The face of* BRACKEN *remains behind its grille of iron.* JOYCE *stands, hands behind his back, as if manacled.*

Dearest Margaret, tomorrow is the day of our severance and final union. I never asked you if you wished to receive a letter from me after my death. But now I write, knowing your wishes, if unexpressed. As I move nearer to the edge of Beyond, my confidence in the final victory increases. How it will be achieved I know not. Does it matter? As surely as I know that you and I are finally one so I know that this world will be redeemed. May Christ Jesus guard you, Margaret, on this day and until he unites us in the bosom of His father. (*Head down*)

The LADY JOURNALIST *comes forward again. As she speaks the light finally goes down on the faces of* BRACKEN *and* JOYCE.

JOURNALIST What I remember most, from the trial of William Joyce, when justice was done, was not that small,

89

slight man with his ridiculous teutonic bow to the judge, nor the palpable relief of the Londoners that he was not to escape, nor indeed the bombed, blitzed city streets outside, no. What I remember was the group of young fascists, the acolytes, the loyal ones, the young men in the gallery, those pale, blue faces, their dark, shining eyes, that look of inspired poverty, inspired promise. They were weeping. Those lilting Celtic voices in grief at the death of their christus. They put on their old raincoats, like vestments, and talked raucously of patriotism. It was as if they had taken the idea of England to some terrible logical meaning of their own which England itself could never tolerate. And before they left in the rain for some secret meeting, some illicit upper-room, the tears poured down those long, emaciated, Celtic faces. They wept for Joyce. They wept for England.